PANORAMIC
DREAM ANALYSIS

A Step-by-Step Guide to Discovering the
True Meaning of Your Dreams

By
Dr. Richard Nongard
Author of *The Seven Most Effective Methods of Self-Hypnosis*

Panoramic Dream Analysis: A Step-by-Step Guide to Discovering the True Meaning of Your Dreams

Dr. Richard K. Nongard

ISBN: 978-1-7344678-9-5

Copyright © 2023 Dr. Richard K. Nongard

All Rights Reserved.

All rights reserved. No part of this publication may be reproduced, distributed, or transmitted in any form or by any means, including photocopying, recording, or other electronic from the author, except in the case of brief quotations embodied in critical reviews and certain other non-commercial uses permitted by copyright law.

First Printing: February 2023

Imprint: Subliminal Science Press

Dr. Richard K. Nongard
1251 Pin Oak Rd. Suite 225
Katy, TX, 77494
(702) 418-3332

www.PanoramicDreams.com

www.ExpertHypnosis.com

Dr. Richard Nongard is available to speak at your business or conference event on a variety of topics. Call (702) 418-3332 for booking information.

Why Read This Book?

This book teaches you the easy-to-follow methods of dream analysis that Dr. Richard Nongard has taught countless others over his 30+ years as a professional psychotherapist.

Imagine not only learning the true meaning of your dreams but being able to understand them from a panoramic perspective so that you can find the important connections to your relationships, your actions, and your emotions.

This book reveals a highly effective step-by-step process based on the psychology of dream analysis that you can master quickly and easily! The best part? By learning how to do Panoramic Dream Analysis and use the HEART process of dream interpretation revealed in this book, you can do away with the one-size-fits-all approach found in dream dictionaries or dream encyclopedias and decipher the unique messages in your dreams.

This book contains the tools you need for self-analysis of your dreams, including simple-to-follow worksheets and detailed directions for becoming an expert in deciphering the symbols and visions from your sleeping mind in no time.

You spend a third of your life sleeping, now use that time to improve your overall well-being as this book reveals the methods psychologists, therapists, professional dream analysts, and even the ancient mystics of spiritual traditions have used to interpret dreams.

Whether you're having trouble deciphering a dream, trying to heal from a traumatic event, trying to stop intrusive nightmares, or learning to create happiness and improve your relationships, this book has the tools you need to unlock the secrets of your dreams and find answers for your daytime world.

Dr. Richard Nongard is America's #1 leading self-hypnosis expert and the author of the bestselling book *The Seven Most Effective Methods of Self-Hypnosis*. His self-hypnosis video and audio sessions have been used by hundreds of thousands of people to create lasting change, and his YouTube sessions have been viewed by millions!

Dr. Richard Nongard is a Licensed Marriage and Family Therapist and an ICBCH Certified Professional Hypnotherapist. His books on counseling, hypnosis, and business leadership are bestsellers in their categories. He holds a master's degree in counseling, an MBA in Business Marketing, and his doctorate in leadership focused on cross-cultural engagement. He is also currently in the dissertation phase of his second doctorate, a Doctor of Psychology degree, where he has focused his research on dreams. He lives in Texas with his family and three Goldendoodle dogs.

Also Get the bestselling self-hypnosis book from Dr. Richard Nongard from your favorite book retailer:

The Seven Most Effective Methods of Self-Hypnosis: How to Create Rapid Change in Your Health, Your Wealth, and Your Habits

Access the free resources that accompany this book at: PanoramicDreams.com

Written by a Leading Expert with 30+ Years' Experience

Dr. Richard K. Nongard is an ICBCH Certified Professional Hypnotist, a Licensed Marriage and Family Therapist, and an expert in helping people create lasting success. He has been a TEDx speaker, he is a popular author with over 29+ books to his credit, and his self-hypnosis videos have been seen by more than four million people.

Dr. Richard K. Nongard is the expert other professionals come to study with and learn advanced methods of professional dream analysis. In this book, he reveals the strategies that actually work and how you can do them at home. Everything is explained step-by-step. When you are finished with this book, you will have a new resource that you can tap into for the rest of your life.

Do you want Dr. Richard K. Nongard to be the motivational speaker at your next event?
Call (702) 418-3332 or visit PanoramicDreams.com

Table of Contents

Foreword by Bob Martel 1

Chapter 1 : The Power of Dream Analysis 7

Chapter 2 : Roadblocks to Dream Discovery 15

Chapter 3 : The Panoramic Perspective 21

Chapter 4 : HEART - Step One: Highlighting 29

Chapter 5 : HEART - Step Two: Explore Emotional Content 35

Chapter 6 : HEART – Step Three: Analyze Archetypes, Symbols, and Imagery 43

Chapter 7 : HEART – Step Four: Rehearsal 53

Chapter 8 : HEART - Step Five: Test, Transfer, Trust ... 59

Chapter 9 : HEART Process Dream Diary Worksheet ... 67

Chapter 10 : Panoramic Views of Our Dreams 71

Chapter 11 : Good Sleep Creates Good Dreams 77

Chapter 12 : Self-Hypnosis and Panoramic Dream Analysis 83

Chapter 13 : Metaphors in Our Dreams 93

Chapter 14 : Free Association in Dream Analysis 99

Chapter 15 : Discovering Patterns and Connecting Dreams 107

Chapter 16 : Nightmares 113

Chapter 17 : Unlocking the Benefits of Your Dreams .. 121

Foreword

At the outset, I need to confess that reading Dr. Nongard's book, *Panoramic Dream Analysis*, stopped me in my tracks.

Surprisingly, as I was not ready for it, the book challenged me to examine my own thoughts and beliefs about the entire topic of dream interpretation and analysis. While I have always tried to follow my own dreams and encourage others to do the same, up until now I had been more than a bit skeptical about dream interpretation, for the myriad books penned throughout the ages fall short of any true value, in my opinion, at least.

This book is different as it presents insights and challenges that opened my mind, as I hope it does for you as well. Whether your mind is already open to the reality of dream analysis, for whatever you seek to understand better in your own life, or if it is pried shut like a lobster claw, the advice found within the covers of this book will enlighten you, if you'll allow.

What is it that makes the very topic of dreams so fascinating, anyway?

Dreams are the topic of great literature, inspiration and motivation, from Henry David Thoreau's famous quote, *Go confidently in the direction of your dreams! Live the life you've imagined,* to William Shakespeare's famous line in Hamlet, *To sleep, perchance to dream,* to Walt Disney's *All our dreams can come true, if we have the courage to pursue them.*

Looking further back, the dream oracles of ancient Egypt, Greece and Mesopotamia entered the world of the dreamer through sleep temples, for healing powers and visioning the future. As a sleep coach, I am fascinated by the evolution of sleep as a healing modality of the mind and body. Dr. Nongard takes us in to the realm of dreams to do the same.

As we know, dreams can be spiritual in nature, as the Bible so clearly reveals in so many examples. Many believe that God reveals powerful messages in our dreams, sent by angels. Our challenge then lies in understanding the meaning found in these dreams, and in taking right action to courageously fulfil the dreams we find so meaningful.

At the intersection of life and death, on this journey we all face in seeking meaning and clarity of purpose, striving for a more meaningful and fulfilling life, we encounter vivid experiences along the way; in our mind, through our imagination, and in reality through daily living.

Panoramic Dream Analysis

Dr. Nongard's book, *Panoramic Dream Analysis*, leads us on a journey of dream interpretation using a distinct and unique process for nurturing our own deeper understanding of what our mind creates during sleep, and perhaps during our lucid, more consciously aware dream states, or even in self-hypnosis.

As the Buddhist story goes, long ago in ancient times, a renowned Zen master by the name of Ryutan was visited by a scholar, Tokusan, who had traveled far to meet with him, with a request to be his teacher. He was seeking greater Zen wisdom and enlightenment, yet it was well known that Tokusan was quite full of his opinions and knowledge about the dharma. He repeatedly interrupted Ryutan with his own stories, revealing his closed mind. Tokusan was unaware that he was not allowing himself to receive the insights being offered by the Zen master, his sought-after teacher.

Observing Tokusan's resistance to learning, the Zen master serenely recommended that they pause for some tea. Ryutan poured his student a cup of tea. While the cup was filled to the brim, he kept pouring, as the story goes, until the cup overflowed. The scholar cried out *"Stop pouring, master Ryukan! My tea cup is already full!"*

"Exactly, my point," the Zen master replied, nodding with a grin. *"You see, you are much like this cup — you are so full of ideas that there is no more room - nothing more will fit into the cup. Come back to me with an empty cup and we will continue!"*

Just as is true with any captivating story the mind absorbs, the recipient assigns the meaning and applies it to his or her need for clarity. Dr. Nongard gives us, in this book, a new sense of appreciation and clarity, allowing the reader to see a path forward using his

Panoramic Dream Analysis process for connecting with our dream experiences.

I believe for the most part that only the dreamer can actually interpret their unique experiences during the sleep realm, in the context of their life in the present moment. I believe, too, that we have to view our collective dream experience as a treasure chest of potential insights into the very purpose and trajectory of our life.

Keep in mind, as I see it and perhaps as Zen master Ryutan shared with me in a deep sleep, dreams are mysterious and often carry profound messages, but it is important to remember that not every dream must be interpreted or made into something tangible. As we journey through our dreaming lives, it is essential to recognize that while interpretation and discernment can be helpful tools for understanding our visions, it is also important to allow space and practice non-attachment. When we take a step back, we can gain valuable insight from our dreams.

Thanks to this book, I have emptied my cup an opened new doorway to understanding dreams from a new perspective.

I encourage you now to empty your cup, as Zen master Ryutan instructs, so that it may be filled. I encourage you to open your mind and your heart to explore what your dreams may be telling you.

Allow new ideas about dream interpretation to flow into your mind, even if simply for further consideration down the road. Open yourself up to your dreams, for it is that emotional connection to your vivid imagination that we find our path, our true north.

Let Dr. Nongard show you the way.

Happy Dreaming!

Robert Martel

January 2023

Chapter 1
The Power of Dream Analysis

I woke up and knew that if I didn't take action in response to my dream, everything would stay the same.

The dream was simple. I had walked into my office, and the boxes on the floor were gone, the bookshelf—which was usually in disarray—was organized with each book placed in related categories, and the trinkets were moved from the back to where they could be seen.

In the previous months, I had often walked into my office wishing it was organized, but I'd never dreamed that it actually was.

Afterward, I woke up, let the dogs out, and got my tea from the kitchen. Walking upstairs, I was happy and content. When I walked into my office and saw the mess, I experienced a sense of disappointment that it was only a dream.

Later on, my subconscious mind reminded me of the disappointment I felt when I realized the organized office was just a dream. I vowed to turn my dream into reality. I had a feeling of determination and motivation to finally accomplish something I knew I could do. It took me about an hour to complete my task, but when I stepped back and surveyed my work, it looked almost exactly like it did in my dream!

Even though this was a simple dream, it's evidence that dreams can be used as a source of inspiration for personal growth or change. Dream analysis can be beneficial for getting an understanding of our subconscious mind and helping us make decisions in our lives. It can also be used as a tool to help recognize patterns and thought processes that we may not have been aware of. Thus, by taking action based on the emotions or sensations that come from dreams, it's possible to move forward with purpose and create the life you want.

Dreams are a source of creativity and inspiration and are filled with meaning and depth. Dream analysis has helped me uncover what I need to focus my energy on and take action on in order to achieve my goals. This simple dream gave me the motivation I needed to act on something I had wanted to do for so long, and I am grateful for it because it pushed me out of my comfort zone and allowed me to grow into a better version of myself. If you ever feel stuck or unmotivated, don't be afraid to turn to your dreams for direction.

Panoramic dream analysis can help you with both the big and the little things in life. It's an approach to acting on your dreams, discovering the meaning of dreams, and examining the content of dreams. People who learn to use panoramic dream analysis do more than just "clean house." They also unlock the potential of our subconscious minds to help us find clarity and create a better future. It can change relationships, untangle complicated emotions, and even transform your habits, your health, and your career. Ultimately, panoramic dream analysis can be a gateway to experiencing the most fulfilling life possible.

When I process my dreams, I often look for patterns or symbols that represent something in my waking life. This helps me gain insight into what could be causing unhelpful behavior or enhancing helpful habits. By reflecting on these insights and turning them into actionable steps, I'm able to make meaningful changes in my life and reach my goals. With this method of working with dreams, it's possible to take control of your destiny in ways you never thought were possible! Dream analysis entails more than just deciphering the significance of our dreams; it also involves acting to bring about positive change in our lives so that we can lead the lives we want to lead.

We can recognize and act upon emotions that come from our dreams, allowing us to move forward with more purpose and intent than ever before. So if you ever feel stuck or unmotivated in life, don't hesitate to tap into your dreams for guidance!

How powerful are dreams? When you're dreaming, no one can tell you that what you're doing is impossible! By transferring the breakthrough of our dreams into the daytime world, you can accomplish almost anything. This is important: the same you that was dreaming is the same you that's now reading this book. The nighttime you is the real you, and your unlimited potential can be unlocked by using dream analysis to gain insight into what your subconscious mind is trying to tell you.

Consider these great accomplishments, all as a result of dreams:

Dmitri Mendeleev, known for formulating the Periodic Table of Elements, struggled to discover a way to organize all the known elements into a meaningful system. As a chemist, he knew that the elements should fit into a grid with certain properties, but after many nights of frustration, he finally gave up. On one particular night, Dmitri had an incredible dream in which he saw all the elements fitting neatly into rows and columns on what appeared to be a giant card file. He awoke from his dream renewed with energy and quickly sketched out a table of elements as it appeared in his dream—the same layout still used today!

In 1817, Mary Shelley had a nightmare about Frankenstein's monster coming to life due to electricity. Intrigued by her own imagination, she crafted the iconic horror story we now know as *Frankenstein*. Indeed, dreams can inspire us to take action and create something wonderful—even if it's a bit frightening.

Larry Page literally dreamed up Google! As an undergraduate student filled with anxiety about remembering everything, he had a dream in which he envisioned all the hard drives accessible from any computer. This dream sparked Page's BackRub project, which eventually became the search engine we all know today as Google.

The sewing machine was invented as a result of a dream. Elias Howe had been struggling for months to come up with an efficient method of sewing. One night he dreamed of cannibals who threatened to kill him. He dreamed that they threw spears at him that, oddly, had holes in the ends. He woke from his nightmare realizing that a machine that featured a needle with the eye at the point and a shuttle carrying the thread underneath it would be required to make the thing work. He figured out how to make this work in real life and patented it in 1846!

These examples show us that when we become aware of our dreams, they can help us unlock vast amounts of creativity and potential. There's no telling what you might create through your subconscious mind if you learn to use panoramic dream analysis, so don't be afraid to explore!

The power of dreams transcends modern times. Since the days of antiquity, dreams have been used as messengers from the gods to help us make decisions and predict the future. They can be a source of great strength and courage or provide comfort in difficult times. It all comes down to understanding the language of dreams and learning how they can guide us in making the right choices to lead our lives with purpose.

Understanding dreams can do more than simply help us create new ideas. They can provide emotional release, transform beliefs, and powerfully answer some of life's most difficult questions. They can inform us about relationships, our life path, and our personal growth.

Dreams can also be a great source of comfort and healing. By understanding their meaning, we can get an insight into current problems and how to deal with them effectively. We're able to tap into our inner wisdom by delving deep into the dream world, which connects us to spiritual guidance and helps us understand existential issues. There is even research into end-of-life dreams and visions, which show us how to better cope with death and dying.

A source of understanding, inspiration, and connection dreams can help us navigate life's challenges and provide much-needed guidance. By taking the time to explore our dreams and work with them consciously, we can unlock their profound potential for self-discovery and transformation. We can open ourselves to new possibilities, free ourselves from limiting patterns, and honor the rich resources within. Dreamwork is an invaluable tool for personal growth and well-being. Through it, we can uncover our own power and wisdom.

Dreams are one of humanity's oldest tools for navigating life. Now, with panoramic dream analysis as a powerful tool at your disposal, you, too, can unlock your full potential. Furthermore, you can use panoramically informed dream analysis to aid in unlocking even more insight into yourself and creating meaningful, actionable steps toward achieving your goals.

When you master the simple process of panoramic dream analysis in the pages of this book, you will uncover your greatest level of creativity. You will learn how even mundane dreams can have value and meaning, and you will finally decipher the messages in your sleep. In so doing, you will become part of a select group of people. Most people never learn to use their dreams to enhance their health, wealth, and happiness, instead chalking up dreams as nothing more than random chance or even superstition. But if you choose to use this knowledge, it can be a powerful tool for personal growth and development.

In this book, panoramic dream analysis refers to the outcome of our processes. What is taught in this book will give you a wide-angle view of who you are and how your dreams can help you live a life that is more meaningful, fulfilling, and in alignment with your true purpose. It will also introduce techniques for effectively interpreting your dreams so that you can use the insight obtained to view your relationships, emotions, beliefs, connections, and life direction from new perspectives.

The process of this analysis is called the HEART process, and it is a step-by-step framework for gaining a panoramic view. The HEART process is the mechanism for attaining a panoramic dream analysis and consists of five steps focusing on easy-to-understand principles and tools. These steps lead you to a wide-angle view, where you can see yourself in the context of your dreams, the connection between your dreams and others, and even discover patterns in the occurrence of particular dream experiences.

The tools of panoramic dream analysis are simple and easy to learn, but they provide a lifetime of benefits. With them, you will understand your deepest desires and how your dreams can help inform your decisions in life and become aware of potential opportunities or dangers that may lie ahead. Furthermore, you'll have access to an inner sanctum that provides a much deeper understanding than simply interpreting symbols or trying to assess what might happen next. By applying these techniques with self-awareness, you can achieve wisdom from within and make positive changes in your life!

It's time to take charge of your subconscious and allow yourself to explore its depths with panoramic dream analysis. Unlocking this knowledge will provide a way for you to access more of your creativity, harness powerful messages from within, and have a better understanding of what your inner self is trying to tell you.

Chapter 2
Roadblocks to Dream Discovery

Do you ever wake up with a smile on your face knowing you had powerful dreams, yet just minutes later, you can't remember anything about the vivid collection of images, conversations, and emotions you experienced? While people think that not remembering dreams is unique, we actually forget a lot of things that vie for our attention during the day. Have you ever gone to the supermarket just to buy one thing and emerged with an entire basket of items, only to get home and realize you forgot the one thing you went to the store for? Far more interesting than the phenomenon of forgetting our dreams is the phenomenon of forgetting most of what we need in life!

The ability to remember and interpret our dreams is something many of us struggle with. Although the amount of detail you can recall naturally decreases over time, it's still one of the main issues holding us back from spending time paying attention to our dreams. Many people mistakenly think that they just do not dream. But studies show that all of us dream every night, typically for two or more hours every night, even if we do not recall our dreams. And why do we forget our dreams? We don't always remember our dreams because the process of sleeping and dreaming is the body's way of detoxifying, healing, and restoring itself. During this process, we disconnect from our conscious minds, allowing us to file the information our brain is processing. Once filed, there's no reason for the mind to return to that memory, with our brains literally choosing to focus on what's in front of us rather than a task it understands as already accomplished.

How can you begin cultivating greater dream-recall abilities? First, just start paying attention to them with purpose, asking yourself every time you wake up what your dreams were. Immediately writing down your dreams in a notebook near your bed can help you refresh your recall. And practice going to bed with intention—this will help you remember your dreams in the morning. These strategies, along with others, such as dedicating a specific time of day to dreamwork and journaling, can all help you increase your ability to remember and interpret your dreams.

Dreams can provide valuable insight into our life experiences and the emotions we express in our waking world. With a little dedication and effort, we can learn how to use this powerful tool to better understand ourselves and make positive changes in our lives.

You can also boost recall by starting to consciously introduce the act of dreaming into your bedtime routine. Take some time to journal and reflect on what you just experienced, or set an intention before going to sleep that you will remember your dreams. When you wake up, take a few moments to lie still in bed and replay the dream images in your mind before trying to move or get out of bed. Also, practice meditation and mindfulness during the day, which are both known to increase dream recall.

By learning to recall our dreams, we unlock the potential for self-reflection in an entirely new way! Dreams are reflections of our inner truth; they provide us with insight into ourselves and help us understand how we feel about certain situations in our waking lives. When we take time to interpret our dreams, we open ourselves up to taking ownership of our dreams.

By taking steps to improve our dream-recall abilities, we can start unlocking the power of our dreams—not only as a way for our unconscious minds to communicate with us but also as a powerful tool for growth, learning, healing, and insight.

Fear can be another factor in finding value in our dreams. Perhaps you've been neglecting your dreams because you're afraid of what they may reveal or what changes the interpretation of them may bring about. This is a very valid fear, but by confronting it, we can learn to embrace our dreams and uncover the valuable information they have to offer. Even nightmares can be valuable. The first lesson we learn from a nightmare is that we wake up from it. That means no matter how distressing a dream is at the moment of dreaming, the dreamer will eventually be safe and secure.

Whether you practice dreamwork or not, one thing is certain: dreams are an essential part of our mental health and well-being, so recognizing their importance and giving them the attention they deserve will be beneficial to us all.

Another reason people do not spend time focusing on the power of dreams is the mistaken belief that dream analysis is superstition or pointless. It's the mistaken belief that dreams have no bearing on or significance in our awake world. The panoramic dream analysis method is predicated on our current research into finding therapeutic value in our dreams. Researchers tell us that those with high dream recall frequency and who understand their dreams report greater emotional stability and higher levels of creativity in their daily lives. So if you want to better understand yourself, your relationships, and the world around you, understanding your dreams can be a powerful way to do just that.

The roots of modern psychology, grounded in the ideas of Sigmund Freud and Carl Jung, come from dream analysis. Both psychiatrists wrote extensively about dream analysis and the value of dreams. Even modern psychotherapies, such as cognitive behavioral therapy, have roots in understanding the value of our dreams to address emotional issues. And, of course, the ancients placed great significance on our dreams, with the Bible in Western culture being filled with dream reports, and the work of the Duke of Zhou and his manual for interpreting dreams dating back over 2,300 years still influencing Chinese and Asian cultures.

Our dreams are important. We know this because we keep having them. And, of course, we know that our dreams are important because, in human biology, nothing happens without a purpose. Our bodies and minds are intricate systems, and our dreams are part of this system. So rather than wasting time worrying about why we can't remember them or what they mean, spend some time really understanding the value of dream analysis and unlocking the potential of your own dreams.

Using a reliable dream interpretation method like panoramic dream analysis is an excellent way to start exploring and understanding your dreams. This systematic approach takes into account all aspects of each dream, including symbols, characters, emotions, interactions, and settings, allowing you to get a comprehensive view of each dream you remember. You can also use tools such as writing journals to document and understand patterns in your dream life over time. Paying close attention to patterns that emerge will help you see the recurring themes in your dreams and allow you to use the information to make positive changes in your life.

Dreams are our innermost thoughts and feelings speaking to us through a language we don't normally understand. They can help us find answers that may otherwise remain hidden, and by understanding our dreams, we can use them as valuable tools for self-discovery and growth. Don't ignore this powerful source of knowledge—take the time to explore your dreams today!

There is yet another shark in the water. Something else holds us back from meaningful dream analysis. That is the plethora of dream dictionaries or dream encyclopedias that purport to tell us what it means when we dream about something. While grand themes in dreams, archetypes, and symbols may have a common core among people or at least within cultures, each dreamer's dream and their own experiences mean that the same dream can mean something entirely different from person to person. That's why it's important to remember that the only reliable way to interpret a dream is through an individual's own personal understanding or through a reputable and systematic method such as panoramic dream analysis which doesn't try to apply a preexisting belief about dream meaning to the dreams you have.

The promise of the panoramic dream analysis approach is that you can use your dreams to get to know yourself, relationships, and the world around you. Therefore it's essential to approach them without relying on preconceived ideas about what each element of the dream could mean. By taking the time to really understand our own unique dreaming patterns, we can unlock a powerful tool for understanding ourselves and charting our paths forward. The result will be a greater understanding of our own innermost thoughts and feelings and a better appreciation for the power of dreaming.

Chapter 3
The Panoramic Perspective

There are two important things to know about dreams. The first is that over eighty percent of the dreams we have are not dreams where we watch a movie about something; rather, they are dreams where we are the actor in a multisensorial experience. What this means is that the "you" in a dream is experiencing the dream as you. In other words, most dreams are from a first-person perspective which means that the emotions, thoughts, sensations, and behaviors in the dream are experienced as if they're really happening.

The second important truth about dreams is that while we often describe them in visual language and from a visual perspective—as if they were movies on a screen—dreams are experienced through all our senses, just like the real world around us in the daytime. Everyone dreams, even visually impaired people. They dream in senses other than sight, such as sound and touch.

In fact, dreaming is usually more vivid than normal waking life because we're not restricted to our normal physical limitations and can travel beyond the bounds of reality. Dreams allow us to explore new and unexplored areas of our minds, experience new people and places, and even visit worlds that we may never have experienced in our everyday lives.

As well as reflecting on ourselves and our environment, dreaming is a tool for problem-solving.

Panoramic dream analysis is so named precisely because the vantage point dreams give us is all-encompassing. There's a panoramic view of the dream experience, the dream analysis is from multiple perspectives, and the outcomes can have broad implications for emotions, relationships, behaviors, life choices, and overall well-being. It can help people gain understanding and create positive change in their lives by exploring the depth and breadth of their dreams.

By looking at a dream from all angles—what happened, who was present, how it felt, and more—panoramic dream analysis enables us to reach into our unconscious and conscious thoughts, behaviors, and emotions. Through this exploration, we can get a better understanding of ourselves and how our lives are shaped by our dreams. This type of dream analysis is not only an interesting way to explore your subconscious but also a powerful tool for personal growth and transformation. By examining each unique dream from many perspectives, panoramic dream analysis can help you achieve a deeper understanding of yourself and the world around you. In essence, it's a way to explore your innermost self in order to create meaningful insight and positive change in every area of life. You might call this the "panoramic perspective."

So how does this work? How do we analyze our dreams and gain these promised perspectives and insights? Let me share with you the stories of two people I have recently had the pleasure to work with in private dream analysis sessions.

The first is a woman who has been struggling with recurring distressing dreams of being taken to a ski lodge. She doesn't ski, doesn't enjoy cold weather or snow, and she was confused about why she'd even have such a dream. But the dream would recur in various forms. Sometimes as a fleeting short dream where her regular mundane dreams were interrupted by the recurring theme of being on a ski lift or at the bottom of a hill. Sometimes she was alone, and sometimes with others. Sometimes the dream would occur as a scene where she arrived at the ski lodge, rented skis, and even took a skiing lesson. The dreams and dream fragments would be mundane to most, but her emotional response to the dream was dissatisfaction, irritation, and stress. She noted that she carried these motions into the following days and wanted to figure out what the dreams meant and how she could stop them.

Through our panoramic dream analysis session, we were able to carefully review each dream fragment as well as explore some of the events in her life that may be connected. We found that while the surface layer of the dream had a physical connection to skiing and snow, the emotional layer of the dream was connected to her feelings of being overwhelmed at work and in life. The ski lodge represented an escape from these feelings of overwhelm because, while she didn't enjoy being in the cold or snow, she did find respite in her dreams at the lodge. The activities she was doing within the dream represented a way for her to navigate that feeling. We explored how she could use other coping mechanisms during times when she felt overwhelmed, and she was able to get an accurate understanding of her dreams as well as create self-empowerment in the process.

The second person I worked with recently was a man who had been struggling with nightmares that he couldn't remember upon waking up. He knew the feelings of fear, terror, and anxiety that accompanied his dream state but couldn't recall the details of his dreams upon waking. Through our panoramic dream analysis session, we were able to explore possible connections between what was happening in his life and what might be causing him the emotional trauma or stress he was experiencing while sleeping.

We found that while the surface layer of the dream may have been connected to terror, fear, and anxiety, the emotional layer of the dream was connected to unresolved issues he had with his family. We were able to explore how he could engage in meaningful conversations about his feelings and experiences during his dreams, as well as create self-empowerment through the process. This was accomplished by using the HEART strategy within panoramic dream analysis, which ultimately led him to be able to not only deal with the emotional content but also to both recall dreams more effectively (giving him a sense of control) and use dream rehearsal strategies to create a new dreamscape for himself. These rehearsal strategies reframed his

Panoramic Dream Analysis

nightmares giving him more control and comfort in his dream state. Soon the nightmares disappeared.

These stories illustrate the power of using panoramic dream analysis to achieve understanding of our dreams. With this approach, we can explore the connections between our dream content and our waking life experiences, as well as use creative techniques to create new dreamscapes that bring us a sense of control and comfort. By engaging with and exploring the content of our dreams, we're able to attain knowledge about ourselves that can help us make decisions and take action in life. With this understanding, we can use panoramic dream analysis to work through issues and develop a deeper understanding of ourselves. Ultimately, this approach can help us acquire insight into our dreams, enabling us to make meaningful changes in our lives.

As mentioned previously, at the center of the panoramic dream analysis process is what I refer to as the "HEART" method. HEART is an acronym for each of the steps in the process, and this process can be used in either therapeutic settings where a professional therapist, coach, or dream analyst is helping you to explore your dream or on your own as a self-guided exploration.

The HEART method of dream analysis is a five-step approach based on the following:

1. **H**ighlight the who, what, when, and how: Take note of who is in the dream, what is happening, when it happens, and how it comes across. Share the dream from a first-person perspective as if it were happening. In hypnotic phenomena, this retelling and noting of the details produce revivification which can help to uncover deeper meanings.

2. **E**xplore the emotional content of the dream: How did the dream make you feel? After all, the meaning of a dream is ultimately determined by how it makes us feel. Emotions are important clues to understanding and can be reflective of how you feel about yourself or a situation in your life that may need attention. We can also look at the emotions of other characters in the dream and what they may represent.

3. **A**nalyze the archetypes, symbols, and imagery: Start breaking down symbols in your dream, as these are often referred to as archetypal images that speak to our subconscious mind. Look for common themes such as messages from the past, fears, or wishes. Focus on the metaphors and symbols in your dreams to gain further insight. In hypnosis, we use metaphors to speak to the subconscious; dreams are almost a form of self-hypnosis where the metaphors of our sleep speak back often with answers for our conscious mind!

4. **R**ehearse: Dreams give us an opportunity to reframe the past, take action in the present, and change our future. Rehearsal is the mechanism for success. Nightmares can be viewed as an opportunity to confront our fears and anxieties. We can use imagery to shift perspective, reframe the situation, or even explore different outcomes in the dream environment. Dreams give us a chance to rehearse communication with others, emotional responses, or physical challenges. They are also a chance to tap into our inner creativity, and the rehearsal stage allows us to map our nighttime experiences into daytime success.

5. **T**est, transfer, and trust: After exploring the dream content, we can revisit the dream and allow it to flow

freely. Notice any changes from the original version of the dream, as this can provide a new perspective or insight into what was originally presented. After rehearsing alternative responses, it's time to transfer this insight into your waking life. Analyzing your dreams can reveal hidden emotions or conflicts that you may be unaware of on a conscious level but still exert influence over your behavior, thoughts, and emotions. Most importantly, trust your intuition about the meaning of your dreams; let go of any preconceived notions or expectations that you may have had going in. Dream interpretation is deeply personal so trust yourself! What you think a dream means is exactly what your dream means.

By following these steps, you can use the HEART method to benefit from a deeper insight into your dreams and draw meaningful connections between them and aspects of your life today—both conscious and unconscious ones! Not only will it facilitate self-discovery, but it can also help you identify patterns in your behavior and provide a better understanding of yourself. As you delve more into the dream world, you may even develop an awareness of how dreams influence your waking life and how to use them as a tool for personal growth.

The HEART method is viewed through a panoramic lens providing the dreamer with a newfound ability to explore and understand the dream world. By diving deep within the subconscious with this technique, it's possible to get a greater insight into oneself and how you interact with the world around you. With this knowledge, an individual can take positive steps toward personal growth and development. Ultimately, panoramic dream analysis can lead to a better understanding of our place in the world and how we can better interact with ourselves, our environment, and other individuals.

By applying the HEART method to dream analysis, it's possible to begin to understand the messages of our subconscious mind so that we can take meaningful steps toward achieving our goals and dreams.

Join with me in the next section of this book, where I'll teach you how each of these five steps in the HEART process can give us a panoramic viewpoint. We'll explore how to interpret dream symbols, use different techniques to access the unconscious mind, and develop creative strategies for making sense of our dreams. Together we'll take a deeper look at the power of dreams and how they can unleash a hidden potential within us. This is your invitation to enter an exciting journey of self-discovery through panoramic dream analysis!

Chapter 4
HEART - Step One: Highlighting

The process begins with highlighting the who, what, when, where, and how of the dream.

In one of my most recent dreams, I was flying on an old 737 in what was supposed to be first class but ended up being a seat no different from the rest of the seats. I experienced the dream from a first-person perspective, and the plane was full of people I didn't recognize. We were taking off from what seemed to be an abandoned airport, and the takeoff was wild with turbulence. As we began ascending, I looked out the window to see the jungle. My seatmate was complaining the whole time and also said something about hating the runway at the airport we were heading to. Since I'd never made this journey before, I was surprised she didn't like the runway. But then, in my dream, I discovered why. The plane descended into the jungle and flying low, I could see that we were landing on a grass airfield that was covered with Bubble Wrap. When we landed, everyone clapped.

This dream can be broken down into its who, what, when, where, and how components:

- The Who of this dream was me accompanied by strangers on the plane.
- The What consisted of me taking off on an old 737 with turbulence and flying over a jungle.
- The When was during the takeoff and as we descended into the jungle.
- The Where was an abandoned airport and a grassy airfield. In my dream, I experienced it as a remote location in the Philippines—a country I have actually traveled to on numerous occasions.
- And the How was us flying low over the jungle to land on Bubble Wrap.

These details are important for further understanding of what the dream may mean.

I want you to notice how I described the dream above. I described it as if I were telling you about something that happened. My description is past tense. I also describe it in the second perceptual position as a narrator describing the dream.

In the HEART process, the highlights of a dream are told from a first-person perspective as if the dream were happening now. If I were doing self-analysis or journaling about my dream, I would write the description differently than I just did. I would write or recall the dream in this way:

Panoramic Dream Analysis

"I am on an old 737. It's supposed to be first class, but the seat feels no different than the rest of them. People I don't recognize are all around me, and we take off from an abandoned airport with wild turbulence. As we ascend, I look out the window and see a jungle below us. My seatmate is complaining the whole time, and she says something about hating the runway at the airport we are headed to. We descend into the Philippine jungle, flying low— maybe somewhere near Mati City. I can see that we are landing on a grass airfield covered with Bubble Wrap. When we land, everyone claps."

This is much different from my first description of the dream. This description is written in the present tense and from my first-person perspective. Telling the dream in this way helps uncover deeper meanings and can help me better understand what my subconscious could be trying to tell me. It also does something hypnotic. It revivifies the experience. In hypnotherapy, "revivification" refers to the process of using sensory detail to bring the dream back to life. This can help uncover symbolic meanings and provide insight into a person's inner state. By retelling the dream in this way, I am reviving the experience and bringing it back to life. Essentially, I am reliving it.

What this process of verification does is it brings back the emotional content, it helps provide recall, and it can be part of the inductive process for the rest of our steps in the HEART process.

It also serves as a reminder that storytelling is essential when it comes to understanding dreams and hypnotic phenomena, so being mindful of the details and retelling the dream from a first-person perspective can help unlock the meaning that lies within.

In the first step, if you are a dream facilitator helping another person, you will find describing the highlights of the who, what, where, when, and how aspects to be an essential strategy. If you are doing self-analysis, you will find by writing in your dream journals from this perspective makes a huge difference.

Each one of the who, what, where, when, and how components is important to flesh out in the first step. In many sessions with clients, they have reported only the ones that stood out. Perhaps the who and immediately began to wonder why that person was there or who that person was.

One interesting thing to note is that we often dream about people, and research shows that the people we dream about are most likely those we have encountered in our real world. In other words, if you dream about going into a store, the clerk in your dream is likely a clerk at another store you actually shop at or your long-estranged former lover or the neighbor who lives next to you! It's a natural inclination of our dreams to put real people in odd places. It's also our natural inclination to get stuck at these points of curiosity and start moving into other stages of dream analysis without exploring all five aspects.

The five elements are not just a tool to help analyze our dreams, but also an effective way to uncover and explore the meaning of our subconscious. By taking note of all the details during dreaming or analyzing a dream, we can begin to unravel the story behind it and come closer to understanding its true message. With practice and patience, we can start to uncover the hidden meanings behind our dreams and make sense of what's happening in our subconscious mind. It's for this reason that it's important not to proceed to step two until sufficient time has been spent on step one.

Practice:

Write a description of one of your recent dreams, highlighting each of the who, what, when, where, and how aspects. Write the dream from a first-person perspective as if you are experiencing it. In other words, rather than writing what you dreamed about, write the dream out as if you're narrating your own experience right now. Even a brief first-person description of who, what, when, where, and how can provide you with a great starting point for practicing this process:

_____
_____
_____
_____
_____
_____
_____
_____
_____
_____
_____
_____
_____

Chapter 5
HEART - Step Two: Explore Emotional Content

The second step in the process is: Explore the emotional content of your dream.

Dream Journal Entry:

I am sitting on a couch. There's a rug with every color in it. The sun is shining in, and I'm surrounded by a peaceful calm. I feel relaxed and content. Suddenly, the room starts to fade away until all that remains is me standing on a vast prairie filled with tall grass swaying in the wind. The sky is a brilliant blue with no clouds as far as I can see.

In the distance, I notice something soaring through the air. It's an enormous eagle! Its wings stretch across the horizon, its feathers like stars scattered throughout the sky. It swoops down and lands right next to me, so close that I can feel its breath on my face. We make eye contact, and suddenly, we are connected.

The eagle speaks to me telepathically, telling me to just be.

The eagle then takes off into the horizon leaving behind its message for me to take with me wherever I go. As it fades away, I wake up, realizing there are no birds in my room.

Chances are pretty good that the dreams you remember best are the ones where you experienced intense emotions (both positive and uncomfortable emotions) or dreams that, when you woke up, you reacted to emotionally. There isn't really such a thing as a bad or negative emotion—each one has worth, all are likely normal, and all have a specific function. People make a mistake when they view depression, anger, or other similar emotions as bad. By doing so, we create a sense of shame around having these feelings, which can cause them to linger and compound the issue. Our challenge is learning how to use the "negative" emotions in a resourceful way.

At this stage of the process, we are simply noting the emotional content of dreams and the emotional response to dreams.

When exploring your dream, take note of the feelings and emotions that you experienced within it. Do not judge yourself for feeling these emotions, as all emotions have a purpose and can serve to help us grow and understand ourselves better. Write down the feelings or emotions that come up for you in this step, simply listing them without judgment or wondering why they are present. Just acknowledge them and begin to notice any patterns or similarities that arise from your dreams over time. By recognizing these patterns, you can start to shed light on the underlying causes of the dream and see why these emotions may be present in your life. Note that if an emotion is present in your dream, it's also present in your life. Remember the principle from a previous chapter; that the us that's dreaming is the us in the dream. These emotions are real, and acknowledging and even accepting them is key to our success in later steps.

By exploring the emotional content of your dream and then exploring the emotions that arise when you think about your dream, you can start to get a better understanding of the underlying message and energy that are present in your life. Through this process, your dreams can become a source of connection and insight into yourself and your journey.

My client, who wrote the dream journal entry about the eagle, discovered by exploring the emotional content of the dream that there was a feeling of peace, contentment, and comfort in the dream. She also found that she felt connected to the eagle, and it left her with a message of being present in the moment. By exploring these emotions further, she was able to learn how these emotions can guide her journey in life and help her stay connected to herself and grow as an individual.

If you are facilitating this process with another person, suggest to them that they simply create a list of adjectives that describe the emotions they felt in the dream and the emotions they felt following the dream. If you are working through this process in self-analysis, you can do the same thing. It's my belief that dream journals can be a resource for really benefiting from the panoramic dream analysis approach. Your journal entries do not have to be long but take a moment to really reflect on the emotions that you felt during your dream and write them down here. Some common examples could be fear, joy, wonder, anxiety, surprise, disappointment, anger, etc. Just acknowledge the emotions without judgment or even wondering where they come from or why they are present.

By recognizing the feelings and emotions in your dream, you can start to acquire insight into why these emotions may be present in your life. After writing out the list of emotions, take a moment to look for any patterns or similarities between different dreams that could provide further insight. Take your time with this step—it's important to explore all the nuances of your dream that could help provide a deeper understanding.

The emotional content of dreams offers invaluable insight into our innermost selves—by taking the time to explore these emotions with curiosity and nonjudgmental awareness, we can unravel hidden truths about ourselves and our lives. With practice, the panoramic dream analysis approach can be a powerful tool for gaining greater clarity and insight into yourself.

By connecting with the emotions that arise during and after your dream, you can start to understand the underlying message or energy present in your life. Through this process, your dreams become a source of connection and insight, providing a greater understanding of yourself and your journey. Finally, take a moment to reflect on all the insights that have arisen from this step and hold them in your awareness as you move forward.

Some questions you can ask yourself that will help you to uncover the nuances of emotions are:

- What did I feel in my dream?

- What emotions did other people in the dream experience or show?
- How did I, as the dreamer, feel in response to these emotions?
- What emotions did the setting or place of the dream evoke in me?
- What emotions might have been present in the other elements of your dream?

Then explore these questions:

- What emotions were felt immediately upon awakening?
- What emotions did I feel later in the day?
- What emotions did I feel as I recalled my dream?
- What emotions am I feeling now that I have written out my dream?

The client was surprised by how many emotions were really elicited from the dream. She was able to put words to her feelings that she had not been aware of. Through this process, she was also able to better understand her dream and the hidden messages it contained. A list of emotions related to the experience of the dream included joy, fear, surprise, confusion, wonder, and many more. But immediately upon awakening, she felt a conflicting confusion and even a slight fear that the dream was connected to something in her real life. The colorful rug brought about a sense of confusion and even irritation, and the windy day created a feeling of dread.

In looking at the emotions in relation to her dream, she was able to understand that the fear and confusion had their origins in her real-life worries and anxieties. During the process of writing the narrative, she was surprised to notice so many feelings, including a set of feelings that appeared very different upon awakening than during the actual dream. She was amazed to look upon the dream with a new perspective and realize how her real-life worries had taken on such an intense presence in her subconscious.

One of the difficulties people have with this step is discomfort with acknowledging some emotions, viewing them as "bad," or even being scared of what they could mean. Understand that whatever emotions arise, there is no right or wrong. All emotions are valid and worth attending to in order to achieve deeper understanding. So be gentle with yourself as you explore this step, letting go of judgment and allowing the process to flow naturally.

How can you be gentle with yourself during this process?

One way is to take breaks as needed. When writing out your dream and exploring the emotions, it can sometimes become overwhelming or intense. Taking a break from the process can help you to reset and come back with a clearer mind and more relaxed energy. You can also practice mindfulness by making the process of each of these steps a meditation. It helps to simply write your list without attaching meaning or judgment—just noting your emotions rather than heavily reflecting on them at this stage of the process. Finally, remember that the goal of this process is to provide insight into yourself and your journey. Keeping this in mind can help keep you grounded as you explore the emotions arising from your dream.

By exploring the emotions of your dreams with curiosity and nonjudgmental awareness, you can uncover valuable insights into yourself and your life's journey. Taking the time to process and understand these emotions can be empowering. With practice, panoramic dream analysis can be a powerful tool for achieving clarity.

Take your time with this step—it's important to explore all the nuances of your dream that could help provide a deeper perception of yourself.

Practice:

As you write the narration in step one, identify the emotions that were present in your dream, and those you felt after your dream, and those you felt during the narration. Write your list of emotions here:

_____   _____

_____   _____

_____   _____

_____   _____

_____   _____

_____   _____

_____   _____

_____   _____

_____   _____

_____   _____

_____   _____

_____   _____

Chapter 6
HEART – Step Three: Analyze Archetypes, Symbols, and Imagery

Step 3 of the process is: Analyze the Archetypes, Symbols, and Imagery. To begin, we look at the archetypes, symbols, and imagery in a dream. Sometimes dreams are rich with detailed and intricate imagery. Sometimes the role or status of people in our dreams is very clear, and sometimes symbols appear that have decisive meaning. Other times, the imagery in a dream is less defined, people are more ambiguous, and symbols are cryptic and less clear. But one principle is at work here: nothing happens in a dream by accident. If something is in your dream, it's something within you—your spirit, your thoughts, or your subconscious—speaking to you.

In this step, it's important to note that the meanings we ascribe to our archetypes and symbols are often culturally derived. In other words, a snake may mean something bad from the cultural perspective of a western Christian, who may attach a meaning to a snake that is cunning and deceitful. A person from a Chinese worldview or experience who has viewed the snake as a powerful figure in the Shengxiao (Chinese zodiac) may see a snake in their dream as lucky or attribute to the snake the qualities taught in the Shengxiao, which might be ambition, intelligence, or quick thinking.

This is why tools like dream dictionaries or encyclopedias of dream meanings have little value. Yes, there are themes that emerge, and there are commonalities in the meaning of things, but "One man's trash is another man's treasure" very much applies to dream analysis. This is why it's important to note an individual's cultural context or background in order to get a more precise meaning of symbols that appear in a dream.

It's also important to pay attention to words used because the subconscious will often use words with double meanings or ones that are loaded with symbolism. It's also good practice to understand which archetypes we may be carrying around and how they show up in our dreams. This can help us look at themes and images that might have been present in a dream without our conscious recognition. For example, if a person feels they are stuck in their life, they may encounter "the path" as a symbol of their journey through life. The imagery could be anything from doorways to roads, bridges, or even rivers.

In this step of the HEART process, it's important to take time and be thoughtful about what the archetypes and symbols in our dreams mean for us specifically. This is where we can begin to find out underlying truths within ourselves that might be speaking to us through our dreams. We may find answers here or have breakthroughs in understanding patterns that might have been hidden from conscious thought before now.

As a facilitator of dream analysis with clients, I don't tell my clients what their dreams mean. Rather, I help them discover the meaning of their dreams. A principle of effective dream analysis is to listen to others and realize that what they think a dream means is what the dream means to them. In self-analysis, this could be said this way, "If you think a dream means something, it probably does!" In the HEART process, we trust the inner wisdom and the ability of the dreamer to decipher the meaning that's important to them.

The archetypes, symbols, and imagery of a dream are powerful tools for exploring the deeper realms of our subconscious and can help us find our own inner truth. With careful exploration, we may be surprised at the hidden depths that reveal themselves when we take the time to listen to what these symbols from our dreams have to say.

Archetypes

Archetypes are universal images that show up in culture, literature, art, religions, and myths. They represent different aspects of ourselves and can help us learn about our emotional world. Common archetypes found in dreams are the hero/heroine, wise elder or guru, villain or monster, and helper characters like angels or spirit animals. Carl Jung, the founder of analytical psychology, believed these archetypes were part of the collective unconscious that is shared by all people. In his articulation of archetypes, understanding the various roles we play in life and understanding our strengths, weaknesses, fears, and motivations can help us be more self-aware.

The hero's journey is another way of defining archetypes. In this model, the hero's journey is seen as the path of self-discovery and growth. The hero embarks on a quest in search of something they need to find or gain. Along the way, there will be obstacles, tests, and challenges which must be faced before they can reach their destination. This metaphor provides insight into our personal development—where we are and what we need to do in order to move forward. Archetypes from this perspective include the traveler, the helper, the protector, and other characters that appear to help or hinder our progress.

In parts therapy, the idea of archetypes is extremely important. Parts therapy is an approach that views "selves" as distinct parts of one's personality and helps us reach a greater understanding of our inner dynamics. There are three main archetypes in parts therapy: the controller, the protector, and the deprived self. These may be expressed in different therapeutic traditions in similar ways. For example, in transactional analysis, the roles are parent, adult, and child; in Gestalt therapy, the roles are persecutor, victim, and rescuer. Sigmund Freud expressed these parts as the id, the ego, and the superego. What all these approaches have in common is the underlying understanding that each of these aspects has a role to play in our lives and needs to be understood, integrated, and appreciated.

Dreaming about a wise sage at a temple or an overbearing parent reveal important archetypes. One client I worked with had a dream that included both the wise sage and the overbearing parent. It was very revealing to him that his own inner voice of wisdom (the wise sage) quite often felt overwhelmed by an internalized parental figure—much like in real life!

In the HEART process, delving into the archetypes of our dream can help us discover our deeper emotional world and get an understanding of the stories we tell ourselves. In this way, archetypes are a powerful tool to secure greater self-awareness and enrich our journey of self-discovery.

How do we analyze or even identify these archetypes? It takes some practice and some knowledge of different archetypes. Writing down the dream and then trying to identify which archetypes show up in it can be very helpful. Additionally, comparing the dream with other stories or myths that have similar themes can provide some insight into which archetypes are present in your own dream.

I suggest that if the ideas of archetypes are new to you, you spend some time reading about the hero's journey, parts therapy, or Jungian approaches to dream interpretation. Then take some time to reflect on your own dreams and see which archetypes show up most often in them.

Although it's beyond the scope of this book to go into great detail on archetypes, Jungian therapists have generally viewed these as common themes and you will probably be familiar with many of them:

- Sage: The Wise Counselor
- Trickster: The Mischievous Interferer
- Creator: Creator of New Ideas

- Destroyer: The Source of Chaos
- Innocent: The Soul of Innocence
- Lover: Passionate Connections
- Caregiver: Source of Compassion
- Magician: The Master of Illusion
- Ruler: Authority Figure
- Jester: Source of Humor
- Warrior: Protector and Fighter
- Outlaw: Breaker of Rules
- Explorer: Adventurer of the Unknown

Do you recognize any of these archetypes from your dreams? You probably do! Each of these archetypes can represent different aspects of our personalities. With practice and awareness, analyzing the archetypes in your dreams will become easier and more intuitive. By recognizing these archetypes in our dreams, we can attain insight into the stories we tell ourselves and how these manifest in our lives, getting a deeper understanding of the underlying dynamics in our dreams and how to best integrate them into our conscious lives.

It's important to remember that dreams are a form of self-expression and by taking the time to explore them we can recognize themes, archetypes, and meanings of our dreams.

Symbols

In our dreams, we will encounter many symbols. Symbols in dreams are often representations of our deeper desires, fears, and aspirations. They frequently take the form of recognizable symbols that represent important aspects in our lives. For example, symbols such as a key, a bridge, a diamond, or an owl can have many different meanings depending on the context and the cultural background. When analyzing symbols in our dreams, it's important to be aware of personal associations. For example, if we have a dream involving a key, what does a key represent to us? An opportunity for growth? A way to unlock our potential? A symbol of power and control? By being mindful of these personal associations, we can get an even deeper understanding of our dreams.

Symbols can also be crosses, stars, religious images, animals, or a variety of other images. In their most powerful form, symbols can lead us to profound emotional states, which are often difficult to access in our waking lives. By deciphering the symbols in our dreams, we can learn more about the inner workings of our psyche and develop a deeper grasp of our subconscious.

Imagery

The imagery in our dreams is often the most powerful element, as it can convey a vast array of emotions and ideas. Imagery in dreams can range from the mundane to the extraordinary, from simple shapes and colors to complex landscapes or scenes. By paying attention to the imagery in our dreams, we can achieve an understanding of our innermost feelings and desires.

For example, if you dream about being in a forest, this could be symbolic of feeling lost or confused in life. If you dream about flying through the sky, this could represent a feeling of freedom or liberation from your materialistic pursuits. Dream imagery is often highly metaphorical and can provide clues into deeper aspects of ourselves that are difficult to access while awake. By exploring these images, we uncover hidden aspects of ourselves that may be influencing our lives.

When exploring the imagery in your dreams, take note of any recurring images or settings that may appear in multiple dreams. This can often provide clues into the underlying issues and feelings that are manifesting in your subconscious mind. By becoming aware of these images and themes, we can learn how to better integrate them into our conscious life.

At this point, it's important to remember that imagery may be more than a visual image. It can be any sensorial representation that occurs in our dreams. Make sure that your analysis probes not only for images but also for sounds, tactile sensations, scents, and tastes. In the HEART process, these can be considered part of the total experience and provide important insights. Every piece of information, no matter how small, can add to the overall understanding and interpretation of your dream.

By exploring the archetypes, symbols, and imagery in our dreams, we learn more about our subconscious minds and uncover hidden aspects of ourselves that may be influencing our lives without our knowledge. By being mindful of these personal associations, we can tap into a powerful form of self-expression.

Practice:

What symbols, imagery, or archetypes do you see in your dreams? Think of a dream you recently had and explore these things. You might now know the meaning yet, but list the symbols, imagery, and archetypes that you witnessed in your dream.

_____   _____

_____   _____

_____   _____

_____   _____

_____   _____

_____   _____

_____   _____

_____   _____

_____   _____

_____   _____

_____   _____

_____   _____

_____   _____

Chapter 7
HEART – Step Four: Rehearsal

The HEART process gives us an opportunity to reframe the past, take action in the present, and change our future. A big part of this success comes from the mental rehearsal that dreams provide. Even nightmares can be viewed as a chance to confront our fears and anxieties in a safe environment.

In therapy, image rehearsal techniques are often used to help individuals reframe situations or explore different outcomes in the dream environment. If a person wishes to practice communication with others, emotional responses, or physical challenges, they are able to do so in the dream state. Dreams can also be seen as a chance for us to tap into our own inner creativity, and rehearsal allows us to better understand how we can map our experiences from the night before onto reality. Doing this helps bridge the gap between unconscious thought and conscious action, which is key for personal growth and development.

This rehearsal happens automatically each night. It's one of the primary reasons why we dream. But when we apply intention to our mental processes of rehearsal, it can become a powerful experience.

A client of mine, who was a baseball player, injured another player when he hit a foul ball. Although prior to this event, he often dreamed about scenarios where baseball was being played, after the event, his dreams became more stressful, and on more than one occasion, aspects of the event when the injury happened began to appear in his dreams (and his waking thoughts).

Using panoramic dream analysis, we were able to explore the event from a different perspective and investigate how he could take what happened in his dream world and apply it to the waking world. We focused on learning from the mistakes of this incident and rehearsing how he would handle similar situations differently in the future. Through working with imagery rehearsal techniques, we were able to reframe his experience and create an outcome that was healing for him.

After days or weeks of mental rehearsal, when tasks become difficult or stressful, you're more likely to be equipped with learned habits that can help you overcome challenges in life. The process of repeating a behavior is known as practice, and it's through practice that individuals achieve confidence and eventually master skills they never thought possible before.

For the baseball player, this fourth step in the process was most important. As we worked together, his rehearsal included mental rehearsal of his batting technique as well as rehearsal of his reaction to similar situations. By the end of our work, he felt more equipped and had greater confidence in his ability to effectively handle and slay difficult scenarios both on and off the baseball field.

Rehearsal is an essential tool for success. It provides us with the opportunity to tackle even our most challenging dreams head-on and find new ways to use dream content to create a better reality. When we incorporate rehearsal as part of our HEART process, it can open up completely new possibilities for growth, healing, and transformation.

This step is not only important when dealing with a specific problem or situation but also for overall personal development. Rehearsal helps us practice different ways of being in the world so that when a challenge presents itself, we're more likely to be equipped with the knowledge and skills needed for success. It's through rehearsal that individuals acquire confidence and eventually mastery over skills they never thought possible before. When done correctly, it can be an incredibly powerful tool for personal transformation.

In working with nightmares, a therapeutic technique called "image rehearsal" is often used to alleviate the stress of these nightmares. The image rehearsal technique involves writing down the nightmare in detail and then reimagining it with a more positive outcome. This can be done by either changing the setting of the dream or using imagery to explore different outcomes that address the fear being experienced in the nightmare.

In the dream journal, we can write alternatively and construct resourceful emotions. We can practice deep breathing and other techniques that stimulate a sense of safety. This process helps us to reframe the dream, take action in the present, and create positive outcomes for our future.

Rehearsal can provide many benefits, both emotionally and mentally. For example, it can help alleviate stress from nightmares, increase self-confidence, provide insight into challenging situations, and ultimately help individuals reach their goals in life. Rehearsal offers a unique way to explore creativity as well as practice effective communication strategies. As we work through each step of the HEART process, it's important to remember that rehearsal is an essential tool for success when used correctly. It offers individuals an opportunity to tap into their inner resources and fully immerse themselves in mapping over to the daytime the learnings from the nighttime.

When I'm facilitating dream analysis with others, in this fourth step, I spend a lot of time helping my clients find the skills our dreams are telling us to develop and practicing developing alternative outcomes. Have you ever noticed that dreams often seem to be incomplete? Almost as if the movie has no ending? This stage allows the dreamer to literally write the ending they want to experience and then practice the dream with the new ending.

I frequently use hypnosis at this stage: having a client recall the dream, revivify the dream, and then reconstruct the dream, but this time all the way to the end. This allows the dreamer to create a new outcome and practice it as if it were real. By using hypnosis to rehearse this new ending, they can bring the changes they made in their dream into reality. It's amazing how many clients go home from a session and then actually redream the dream with the new ending. It's powerful to watch the dreamer take control of their dream and recreate what was once a nightmare into something that brings them empowerment.

Rehearsal is an incredibly important step in the HEART process. It provides us with the opportunity to reframe our situations and explore different outcomes to ultimately create positive change in our lives.

In self-analysis, you can use the idea of rehearsal as a strategy by engaging in imagination and visualization to replace old negative behaviors or thought patterns with new positive ones. This can be done by constructing a mental image of the desired behavior, feeling, or outcome and mentally rehearsing it until you are comfortable with what you want to achieve. The more detailed the scenes are and the more often it's repeated, the more successful the rehearsal will be. Rehearsal is an important part of self-reflection as well as for reflecting on difficult situations that have happened in our lives. We can use rehearsal as a tool to envision what could have been different and how we would handle things differently next time. We can also use this technique to explore creative solutions to challenging problems rather than simply relying on past experiences or old ways of thinking.

Simply setting aside time during the day, even a five to ten-minute break, to practice your dream rehearsal is all that self-hypnosis or dream meditation entails. During this time, you can imagine yourself as the hero or heroine that exists in your dreams and then visualize any positive change that you would like to see happen in your life.

This is a great way to build self-confidence and cultivate the capacity for positive change in our lives.

Ultimately, rehearsing is an important part of the HEART process because it allows us to explore different possibilities while still maintaining control of our experiences. Through practicing different outcomes, we can create more successful solutions and move towards greater personal growth and well-being. Rehearsal also helps us tap into our creativity, develop communication strategies and increase self-confidence—all key components of success when working with our dreams!

Practice:

Now ask yourself what the dream is trying to tell you. By reviewing your dream in this way—as a retrospective—you put some space between yourself and the emotions. You can literally rehearse options and outcomes, changing the dream content at this stage and seeing it as an opportunity to problem-solve. Spend some time reflecting on this question and wait for an answer to come through. You can also spend time journaling or even meditating on this inquiry if you would like. Identify and write down what you feel the dream is trying to tell you:

_____

_____

_____

_____

_____

_____

Chapter 8
HEART - Step Five: Test, Transfer, Trust

After we have explored the previous steps, revisited the dreams, and noticed any differences from the original version and even expanded on the dream, the final stage of the HEART process allows us to evaluate how the process resonates with us. It gives us the ability to transfer our learning to our daytime actions and finally teaches us to trust our dreams.

In this final stage, the goal is to map over as a resource our analysis of our dreams into daytime actions. We can test our dream content by asking ourselves questions such as "How does this knowledge impact my life?" and "Does this insight help me to better understand myself and the challenges I'm facing?"

Once we have developed a greater understanding of our dream content, it's important to put these insights into practice in order to get concrete results. Looking at how we can apply the information that was gained from our exploration of the dream in our waking lives allows us to make tangible changes that will benefit us on an emotional, mental, or physical level. This could be as simple as noticing patterns or triggers that cause heightened emotions and working through them with alternative responses rather than giving in to negative reactions. Ultimately, trusting your dreams is vital for being able to transfer your understanding and apply it in everyday life. Your dreams provide an insight that you may not be able to access through conscious thinking, so believing in the power of your subconscious can aid you in finding greater awareness and control over your emotions and actions. With practice, by applying the HEART process, we can learn how to better understand our dreams and use this knowledge to make positive changes in our lives.

The HEART process provides a framework for exploring dream content that can be used with any dream or recurring theme. Through allowing yourself time to explore the dream content with no judgment or assumptions of meaning, recognizing patterns or triggers that cause heightened emotions, practicing alternative responses to challenges faced, testing for tangible results, and ultimately trusting your dreams, you have the ability to further understand yourself and your own behavior.

In exploring my own dreams, I used this process to analyze a dream that I recently had. In the dream, I was in a large maze-like garden and felt like I had been following a path that led me in circles with no way out. I recognized this to be a representation of feeling lost, overwhelmed, and unable to find my own way. By using the steps of the HEART process, I explored these feelings further and understood that they stem from feelings of insecurity and fear of failure when presented with new challenges. This final step allowed me to transfer my interpretations into actual practice by reminding myself to take things slowly, ask for help if needed, and believe in myself even when facing unfamiliar obstacles. I responded to the dream by testing it—asking myself if this really was the meaning of the dream and comparing my feelings to other situations I have found myself in.

I transferred my analysis to the real world by vowing to take my time with any challenge presented and trust the process. I reached out to a friend who I knew had faced a similar situation to mine, and the new understanding of myself and the message of my dream was one I grew to trust.

Through repeating this process, I was able to get more clarity on my emotions and reactions and ultimately use this knowledge to better understand myself and make meaningful changes in my life. The HEART process serves as an effective way of accomplishing insight into your subconscious feelings, allowing you to see past just surface-level interpretations or misunderstandings of your own behavior. It provides a safe space for further exploration that can lead to greater self-awareness, emotional regulation, and long-term development. Allowing yourself the time to interpret your own dreams can be incredibly rewarding, giving you the opportunity to better understand yourself and make tangible changes in your life.

Consider this dream that came from a dream journal of one of my clients:

I was driving on a highway for hours, and then I noticed the truck I was driving had no gas gauge. It was an electric truck but was a special truck not yet released to the world that was self-perpetuating through solar electricity. I had no idea how long I could drive on it and kept asking for help from people I called, but nobody could help me.

By using the HEART process, my client was able to explore this dream further and realize what it might mean in relation to his life. After examining the dream content, we discovered that the truck represented his journey in life, and not knowing how far he could go with it symbolized a feeling of insecurity about his future.

Through rehearsing alternative responses to challenges faced, he realized that he should take risks despite any fear holding him back and believe in himself even when facing uncertainty. By testing these ideas, he noticed tangible changes occur when trusting his own instincts and transferring this understanding into everyday life. By trusting his dreams, my client was able to understand his behavior and develop greater self-awareness. Ultimately, the HEART process allowed my client to make meaningful changes in their life and take control of their future.

There are three primary strategies that can help out in this part of the HEART process. The first is to test using a principle we can borrow from neuro-linguistic programming; this is the TOTE process, which stands for Test, Operate, Test, Exit. This means that after exploring the dream content and rehearsing alternative responses, it's important to actively test those responses in real-life scenarios. This allows us to gain feedback on whether or not our interpretations were valid and whether we should continue using them. Put some of the learnings from your analysis to the test, operate as if the learnings are working, test them again, and then make a determination about whether this is something you should continue doing or exit.

The second strategy is to transfer the insight from your dreams to your waking life. Dreams often give us valuable information that can help us better understand our own emotions, thoughts, and behaviors. It's important to use what we've learned in order to make tangible changes in our everyday lives and move forward with our newfound knowledge. To transfer to your waking world, you can use a strategy of visualizing and affirming the dream interpretations or insights. To do this, visualize yourself in a situation that mirrors the dream content, affirm your interpretation of it, and then apply it to real-world scenarios.

The third strategy is to trust our dreams. Our dreams are often filled with hidden emotions and conflicts that we may be unaware of on a conscious level but still affect us in meaningful ways. It's crucial to take time to explore these feelings, analyze them, and develop insight that can help us better understand ourselves and make changes in our lives. There is no right or wrong way to interpret your dreams, but ultimately trusting what they tell you can have immense power in understanding yourself further. The best way to trust your analysis is to realize that the dreams are yours; you are the dreamer, and even though it may seem fantastical, we can integrate our nighttime world into our daytime responses.

Notice that this process is far different than just looking up dream meaning in a dream dictionary. This final stage in the HEART process ties together the previous strategies and allows you to attach the meaning that's most important to you. It means that you are discovering solutions from within and are ultimately self-directed and no longer dependent on solutions outside of yourself (the whims of others or the words of a dream dictionary or prophet). Instead, the HEART process helps us understand our dreams and transfer the insight into our waking lives in order to see real-life results.

The key takeaway is that with practice and guidance, you can become familiar with your own thought patterns so that you can begin to trust yourself more and recognize when solutions should come from within. By engaging in this process regularly, you may find that it becomes easier to recognize potential problems before they arise as well as take control of how you choose to respond to challenging situations. Ultimately, the HEART process allows us to make meaningful changes in our lives by giving us greater self-awareness which starts with trusting ourselves and our dreams. This cycle of change is something that can be repeated again and again.

The ultimate goal is to become more aware of how we think and feel, increase our self-trust, and develop better ways of responding to challenging situations. The HEART process can help us achieve this goal by teaching us how to analyze and respond to our dreams in a meaningful manner that will result in real-world changes. We can then use the insights from our dream explorations to make tangible improvements in our lives so that we are living as our highest selves. By understanding the value of dream exploration, we can learn more about ourselves, trust ourselves more deeply, and ultimately pave the way for lasting change.

Practice

Finally, think about how this message can be applied to your everyday life. How can it help you make positive changes so that you can achieve greater personal growth and development? Write down any actions or steps that come to mind here:

_____

_____

_____

_____

_____

_____

_____

_____

_____

_____

_____

Chapter 9
HEART Process Dream Diary Worksheet

The HEART process dream diary worksheet is designed to be a resource for you both tracking your daily dreams as well as outlining elements of the HEART process. My recommendation is that you keep a dream journal in the form of a notebook near your bed. This will make it easy for you to immediately begin tracking your dreams. I've also added a free printable version of the worksheet as a download at my website, which you can access at www.PanoramicDreams.com by simply letting me know where to send the files. You can then print multiple copies at a local copy center and keep them in your notebook.

By tracking your dreams on a daily or at least a weekly basis, you will begin to notice patterns and subtle messages that are being communicated in your dreams. This will help you identify themes and symbols from the dream world, as well as integrate their messages into your waking life.

The worksheet provides some straightforward steps for you to follow in order to review your dream diary entries and practice the HEART process. The goal of this exercise is to become more aware of recurring motifs and archetypes, which can then inform how we interpret our current reality through a deeper understanding of ourselves. By exploring our own personal mythologies, we can access insights that can help us reach our highest potential.

The worksheet also offers some guidance on how to engage with any connections between what was manifesting in your dream and the challenges that you face in the waking state. Doing this will help to bridge symbolic elements of our inner world with tangible goals and intentions in a more conscious way.

Finally, by engaging with the HEART process on a regular basis through the dream diary worksheet, you will begin to notice shifts within yourself on a deeper level. This can be an incredibly empowering experience as you become more aware of how to shape your life according to what's currently arising from your dreams. If you're working with a facilitator or therapist who has suggested this process, you can bring these worksheets to your sessions and be supported by them in exploring the dream world.

The first part of the worksheet is step one in the HEART process. This is where you will highlight the who, what, when, where, and how. These are the details of your dream to the best of your ability. You should be writing in the first person as if the dream were currently being experienced. This will help both with recall and with establishing a sense of presence and awareness during the dream.

Below this step are the remaining four elements of the HEART process, including exploring emotional content, analyzing archetypes, symbols, and imagery; rehearsal; and finally, test, transfer, and trust. There is space on the worksheet to write enough of your thoughts to make it meaningful but also to keep it concise. This worksheet will also help you preserve the dream for later review, and if you're interested in lucid dreaming, it might even be a guide for directing dreams to a deeper level.

The very end section of the worksheet is a reflection section where you're asked to connect the dream or the analysis to any other interpretations that you may have. This is a helpful way to receive any insights or messages from the dream without getting lost in details or suffering from analysis paralysis.

Once you finish this process, it's important to keep track of your progress on the worksheet and review them periodically so that you can connect the dots between what was being expressed in each dream and its significance for the here and now. I suggest revisiting your dream diary at least once a month in order to to get a better understanding of how our subconscious mind is attempting to communicate with us through dreams. You can set aside time to do this, making it a meditation and reflection period.

Ultimately, by engaging with this practice regularly, one can develop their own personal dream language, which will help make sense of both current life circumstances as well as patterns from our past. Using this dream diary worksheet will help you become more aware of what your dreams are trying to tell you and how they can guide you in your present reality.

A final reminder: The dream diary worksheet is an invaluable tool for self-exploration and should not be overlooked or undervalued. It's a powerful way to gain insight into ourselves, as well as our lives and all the influences that shape them. I hope that you enjoy engaging with the HEART process and find it beneficial in your life's journey. Most importantly, listen to yourself, trust your intuition, and enjoy the process.

(Access your printable full-size version at PanoramicDreams.com)

Chapter 10
Panoramic Views of Our Dreams

When we think about a panoramic view, we're imagining a wide and expansive view of the landscape around us. Whether we're standing on top of a mountain looking out over the valley below or standing at the edge of a lake surrounded by trees, panoramic views are breathtaking—leaving us feeling small in comparison to the vastness of nature. Panoramas can also provide a sense of perspective and context when viewing larger pictures from far away, such as cities or landscapes. By seeing how different elements within an area relate to one another, we're able to better understand our environment and appreciate its beauty even more.

In panoramic dream analysis, this wide-angle view allows us to see the bigger picture of our lives, dreams, and goals. By looking at the entire scene with a new perspective, we can gain insight into our subconscious mind and explore how we relate to both ourselves and the world around us. Through this type of analysis, we can learn to identify patterns in our behavior that may be holding us back from achieving our desired outcomes or discover hidden motivations within our unconscious minds. Additionally, panoramic dream analysis can help us uncover information about our relationships with others that may have been previously unknown. By understanding these deeper connections, we're better equipped to make positive changes in our lives and move toward healthier relationships with those around us. With a clearer view of ourselves and the world around us, we can feel more empowered to take control of our destiny and reach the goals we have set for ourselves.

When we take time to explore the panoramic view of our subconscious mind through dream analysis, we have an opportunity to get a deeper understanding of ourselves that can lead to positive change and growth both personally and professionally. As we journey through this process together, I truly believe you will uncover many insights into yourself you never knew existed!

Panoramic is a long word. Nine letters long. In China, that's considered the emperor's number; in Norway, it's frequently used in mythology; and in Judaism, it's the symbolic number of truth. In my experience, panoramic dreams are associated with exploration, emotional clarity, and understanding. By applying the HEART process, you will discover panoramic solutions in every area of life. These nine letters form an acronym that describes the depth, breadth, and beauty of our dreams.

P.A.N.O.R.A.M.I.C. represents the outcome of the HEART process. These nine outcomes are Power, Answers, Nurturing, Overcoming, Renewal, Awareness,

Mindfulness, Insight, and Connection. As you allow the HEART process to guide your exploration of panoramic dreams, may you find yourself in awe of the amazing picture that awaits you. Each component is a reward for spending time doing dream analysis.

Power: Strength is gained from understanding the complexities of our dreams.

Answers: Our dreams provide us with answers to questions we have about our lives and goals.

Nurturing: We can nurture ourselves and our relationships by recognizing behaviors that may be holding us back from reaching our fullest potential.

Overcoming: Dreams can help us identify destructive patterns in our lives so we can begin to move forward.

Renewal: Through dream exploration, we can acquire a new outlook on life which brings about feelings of hope and renewal.

Awareness: By becoming aware of underlying motivations, we more clearly understand how to make positive changes in our lives.

Mindfulness: Being mindful of what lies beneath the surface and being open to looking at things from different perspectives is key to gaining insight.

Insight: By tapping into our subconscious minds, we can achieve a deeper understanding of ourselves and the world around us.

Connection: We can learn more about our relationships with others and uncover hidden connections that may have been unknowingly present.

As you explore panoramic dream analysis, I hope you find yourself in awe of the incredible picture that begins to take shape—just like a panoramic photo—but this time a panorama of good things in your life. The HEART process brings clarity and empowerment as you continue your journey of self-discovery!

By embracing this process and understanding its full potential, you can unlock deeper levels of self-growth and awareness. You will be able to access new perspectives on how to move forward with greater ease and clarity and ultimately have a better understanding of yourself and the world around you. Panoramic dream analysis is an incredible journey—from viewing your life from a bird's-eye view all the way down to exploring every intricate detail contained within these nine letters. The possibilities are infinite!

Yet many wonder if dedicating the time required for dream analysis is actually beneficial. As a facilitator of dream analysis sessions, whether I'm helping a client in therapy, coaching, or even focusing solely on dream analysis, I find that the process creates deeper levels of rapport, engages clients in therapeutic processes, and can also be used to help break through stuck points in the clients' thought processes. Additionally, dream analysis can also reveal much more than initially expected; as we explore the unconscious mind, deeper awareness and understanding can often be revealed that had been previously hidden.

But are there benefits for the client in therapy or for someone practicing a self-directed form of dream analysis? The answer to that is "Yes." Dreamwork can help reduce the severity of distress associated with nightmares. Overcoming this distress is one of the main benefits of dream analysis. The panoramic dream analysis method reduces the distorted importance dreamers have placed on their nightmares and replaces it with a panoramic view that sees the nightmare in the context of a larger picture. Thus the fear of nightmares dissipates, and the dreamer can approach the nightmare in a more lucid and calm manner.

Many of the clients I've worked with over the years struggle with decision-making. They fear making the wrong decision, and they second-guess decisions that have been made. Dream analysis provides a safe and nonjudgmental space to explore their options. By exploring the context of the dream, they can attain clarity and insight into what their goals are, identify patterns that may be holding them back from progress, gain understanding of why certain decisions were made in the past, or better understand relationships they have with other people in their lives. This can help them move forward and make better decisions based on this new awareness.

Panoramic dream analysis also helps us see our dreams in terms of their psychological meanings, enabling us to uncover patterns that are hidden within them. For example, if a person is considering a certain decision they have to make in their waking life, exploring their dreams through panoramic dream analysis may help reveal connections between the dream elements and their thoughts about the situation. This insight can then be used to guide decisions and determine what action should be taken next.

Dream analysis can help with personal growth, self-esteem, and self-acceptance. It can ignite gratitude and give us new tools for interacting with our family, our peers, and our community. Dream analysis can also provide us with a sense of hope, a renewed feeling of purpose, and a better understanding of our relationships.

Do you experience difficulty with certain distressing emotions? Anger? Resentment? Fear? Depression? Dream analysis can be used to explore these emotions and uncover their deeper meaning. By understanding the symbols, emotions, and situations that appear in our dreams, we can obtain insight into the subconscious source of these feelings. It's quite likely that with this newfound awareness comes feelings of greater acceptance of yourself and your circumstances, which can help to improve your mental well-being.

Perhaps one of the best ways to develop emotional intelligence or social intelligence is through dream analysis. In the HEART process, we're able to explore these emotions and understand why they're being experienced. This can often lead to greater understanding of the self and others, as well as increased empathy.

In the next sections of this book, I'm going to share ideas for increasing the panoramic perspective, giving you a wider view of your dreamscape, emotions, behaviors, and social relationships.

You can actually begin fulfilling these promises right now by making a dedicated commitment to trying it for yourself. Analyzing one dream is fun and even interesting, but spending the next thirty days really looking at multiple dreams, discovering themes in these dreams, and finally taking action from the insights gained through them is far more valuable.

Chapter 11
Good Sleep Creates Good Dreams

One of my clients, George, lamented that while he had dreams, he didn't remember them very often. He enjoyed and benefited from the panoramic dream analysis approach and wished that he had more dreams to draw from. Almost like a jealous child, he said, "My wife remembers her dreams every day!" After a thorough assessment of his sleep hygiene, we were able to identify a few areas where changes could be made.

What was the solution? We started by making sure George was getting enough sleep. Sleep deprivation has been linked to memory problems, so increasing total sleep time would help him remember more dreams. We also identified certain lifestyle habits that were contributing to his poor quality of sleep, and worked on reducing or eliminating those behaviors. For example, limiting caffeine intake in the late afternoon and reducing stress before bedtime are two strategies that can help improve the overall quality of sleep.

We also talked about dream recall techniques, such as writing down all possible details after waking as well as keeping a dream journal with regular entries every morning. By intentionally focusing on dreams, my client was able to increase his dream recall rate and get better quality sleep, which ultimately led to more meaningful dreams to analyze.

My mantra has become "Good sleep = good dreams." George took action to improve his sleep and now has a greater understanding of how he can use his dreams as a source of guidance and insight into himself and the world around him. He attributes much of this newfound clarity and understanding to conscious efforts like getting enough sleep, changing lifestyle habits, and utilizing dream recall techniques. All of these steps taken together have resulted in a better night's sleep, leading to more memorable and meaningful dreams.

Factors that can impact sleep quality include:

- Caffeine
- Stress
- Lack of exercise
- Poor diet
- Excessive screen time before bedtime
- Creating an environment conducive to restful sleep (dark, cool room; comfortable bedding, etc.)
- Setting a regular sleep schedule
- Developing pre-bedtime rituals such as reading or listening to calming music

- Limiting naps throughout the day

Research is now showing that one of the biggest impediments to better sleep is screen time before bed. Many of us are used to checking our phones in bed, using a tablet, or even watching TV. These electronic devices prevent us from getting restful sleep because the brightness of the screens tricks our brains into thinking it's still daytime. We know that better sleep leads to better dreams, and being mindful about how we use technology in the bedroom can help us achieve this goal.

Eating habits are also important. It's not just diet but when we eat that's important for regular sleep. Get in the habit of ending your daily eating hours before bedtime, avoiding snacks or late meals. How does this help improve sleep? Eating late at night causes our bodies to work to digest food while we're supposed to be winding down for sleep, so eating earlier in the day and avoiding late snacks can help us get a better quality of sleep.

Evaluate your environment for sleeping. Do you have the same pillows you had two years ago, and they're now lumpy or uncomfortable? A new pillow can be had for as little as $5. Pillows were not really designed to be used forever. The average hotel replaces its pillows every six months. You should too. I've found that a quick trip to the store to refresh or update the bed can also make a huge difference. If your sleep environment is not restful, it might be time to consider some minor updates or adjustments.

For others hoping to experience the same results George did, I recommend taking a comprehensive approach to improving sleep habits. By making small changes in lifestyle and developing techniques for better dream recall, it's possible to get better quality dreams that can be used for personal growth and insight into one's life.

Poor sleep quality can mean difficulty falling asleep, waking up in the middle of the night, or having difficulty staying asleep. All these problems can be addressed with small changes in lifestyle habits.

George's story is proof that good sleep leads to better dreams. He took action and slept more, reporting more frequent dreams that were easier to remember. With a little time and effort, anyone can get on their way to experiencing more meaningful dreams that help them get a perceptiveness of themselves and their lives.

Although George made changes in most of the areas listed above, one technique that I taught him stood out as making the biggest difference. That technique was learning mindfulness meditation. Mindfulness meditation is an approach to calming the mind before sleep and can help reduce stress and anxiety. This practice has been linked to improved quality of sleep, leading to more vivid dreams with greater emotional depth.

How can you practice mindfulness?

The basic principle in mindfulness is that rather than trying to clear the mind, we practice being present with our thoughts, feelings, and sensations and simply accepting them without mentally following them. This can be done through the practice of mindfulness meditation, which involves sitting quietly and focusing on the present moment. Additionally, studies have shown that even just ten minutes per day is enough to experience positive changes in one's mental and physical health and the sleep-related benefits of mindfulness.

To practice mindfulness right now, sit or lie down in a comfortable position and close your eyes. Take some slow deep breaths and focus on sensations such as the air around you, your body touching the surface below you, or the sounds of the environment. Allow thoughts to come without judgment, and gently move your attention back to bodily sensations when they arise.

When I say "without judgment," I mean don't attach importance to the many thoughts, feelings, and sensations you notice, choosing instead to practice returning your attention to the breath. The idea is to stay in the present moment rather than reviewing, regretting, or thinking about the past and not projecting or worrying about the future.

It's our natural inclination to scan the past to predict the future, but the problem with that is we miss the power of the moment. In each moment, we are okay, even if life is stressful. We can be still without tension, and we can release anything known or unknown that's keeping us from getting the most out of our dreams.

A simple script you can memorize can become a bedtime ritual and help you practice mindfulness.

As you sit quietly preparing to sleep, say, "I am aware of my breath, and I accept whatever comes to my mind." Pay attention to the in-breath and pay attention to the exhale. Notice that when the mind wanders, you can intentionally bring the attention back to the breath—each breath marking each moment.

Say to yourself, "I am letting go of my day and preparing for restful sleep."

Say to yourself, "I am grateful for the moments of peace I am experiencing."

Another way to practice mindfulness is to start your day with the same meditation. You can set an intention and practice mindfulness throughout the day by just observing your thoughts and feelings without passing judgment. I suggest that you set aside a specific and easy-to-remember time to do this, and what better way than to take a mindful shower, paying attention to your body, your breath, and your intentions?

We can relax the mind and increase awareness of ourselves and our surroundings by engaging in mindfulness practices. In turn, this will help us sleep better and feed into experiencing better dreams. As George showed with his story, these efforts can lead to clarity and insight into one's life as well as personal growth.

Using some of these strategies could help you live a better life overall if you're looking for ways to sleep better and have more vivid dreams. Whether it's creating a routine around your sleeping habits or incorporating mindfulness practices into your day-to-day life, these strategies can make a big difference. By practicing mindfulness regularly, you can improve the quality of your sleep. And with better quality sleep comes more vivid dreams that are easier to remember. So make sure to practice these techniques if you want to get better dreams.

Chapter 12
Self-Hypnosis and Panoramic Dream Analysis

One of my clients had spent considerable money and time focused on learning dream analysis, even attending a couple of seminars by dream analysts who, in the end, were simply providing a list of images, totems, icons, symbols, and dream topics and matching them to a preconceived encyclopedia of dream meanings. As he said, this was going to be his last attempt at understanding his dreams in a coherent and concise way. To him, learning dream analysis was vital to his well-being and acceptance after the loss of his only son in a horrific accident. Although many years had gone by since the death of his son, he continued to have dreams about him. He wondered if, in fact, these were messages from his son and what the messages meant.

The dreams he had were frequent over the years, and although some might be characterized as nightmares or distressing, other dreams were reassuring and even joyful. He wanted to understand what these dreams meant, and he thought that dream analysis would provide the answers.

In my work with him, the first thing I did was teach him that dream analysis is not as rigid or simplistic as matching symbols to a preexisting set of meanings. I taught him that dream work is fluid and ever-evolving and allows for the development of personal insights into those messages from his subconscious mind. I didn't address whether the dreams were a direct message from his son or not; in my own personal belief system, I'm not inclined to believe in such messages. But what is most important in helping others is to accept the client's experience and beliefs as valid to them, so we kept the door to this possibility open.

One of his recent dreams about his son was narrated in this way:

I was driving my car, and my son was in the back seat. He had a blue elephant toy, and when I asked him about it, he said it was his favorite elephant. I asked him if he wanted to keep it, and he said "Yes." I don't know where I'm driving to, but I know that as long as I'm driving, he's happy with his elephant. He's smiling and playing. I'm driving but looking in the rearview mirror at him. We get to the center of town, and when I park, I wake up.

Narrating a dream, as above, in either written form or by sharing it with a dream analyst, coach, or even a friend in a first-person perspective, is step one in the HEART process. The second step, Exploration of Emotions, allows us to explore and analyze the content of emotions both in the dream and as one revisits the dream later. In this case, the client revealed his main emotions were joy and serenity, and that he felt a connection to his son when having this dream and that driving with his son allowed him to feel closer to him.

The third step, Analysis of the Archetypes, Symbols, and Imagery, allows us to dive deeper into the dream with the objective of discerning possible meanings. In this particular dream, we can explore further what the blue elephant and driving may mean for this client. The symbol of an elephant is often associated with strength, power, and wisdom, as well as protection from danger; that it was blue could suggest peace, calmness, serenity, spiritual healing, or reconciliation.

The fourth step in HEART is Rehearsal. This is a chance to reframe the past and plan the future. This can best be accomplished by connecting back to the emotions experienced in the dream and by considering how these can be applied to our lives. In this case, perhaps it could suggest that reconnecting with his son through the symbolism of the blue elephant is a way for him to remember some of those positive feelings he had when his son was alive and thus help his process of healing and acceptance even further.

The fifth and final step in the HEART process is the Test, Transfer, and Trust process. My client and I discussed how he could apply this dreamwork to his life going forward and that connecting with the emotions of joy and serenity from the dream was a way for him to reconnect with his son. He also discussed that it was crucial for him to trust in himself as he continued on his healing journey and remember the feeling of joy he experienced in the dream.

While the above vignette briefly describes the five steps in the HEART process, what I want to share with you now is how, after our initial meeting, self-hypnosis helped my client to expand on each of these steps, connect his past dreams to his current experiences, get freedom from feeling that he was misinterpreting the dream or missing the messages, and build a deeper understanding of his relationship with this son. In essence, self-hypnosis can be used to open the doorway even further to our own unique personal dreamwork and journey.

Dreams are meant to bring us messages that help us heal and grow in life; with the right tools, such as the HEART process and self-hypnosis, we can access these powerful inner resources more deeply and accelerate our own healing process.

I have written several books on hypnotherapy, and two of my bestsellers are on self-hypnosis. In my book, *The Seven Most Effective Methods of Self-Hypnosis*, I share a self-hypnosis strategy based on autogenic training. Autogenic training refers to the ability to create from within. In the basic strategy of self-hypnosis, we learn to create warmth and heaviness—two physical sensations. But the learning here is that if we can create physical sensations, we can create anything from within. We can create acceptance, confidence, joy, and even a resolution to grief and loss.

It all begins with a basic process in self-hypnosis called autogenic training.

Autogenic training is a confidence-building method of self-hypnosis. It teaches that even the most powerless have ultimate control over what is most important—the body. Perhaps not at the level we hope for, but at some level, we always retain control, and autogenic training teaches this through experience.

With this method, the changes that you experience here will be changes you create from within yourself, demonstrating the power of the mind to fully control our physical responses through the autonomic nervous system. Take the next two or three minutes and guide yourself through this simple process by reading along and focusing on the experience you create.

Practice Session: Autogenic Training

This is a very brief exercise based on the longer protocol for autogenic training.

Sit in your chair in a posture that promotes awareness and comfort, with your spine straight and your feet on the floor.

Begin by closing your eyes and focusing your attention on your hands.

As you relax, focus on your hands and say to yourself out loud, "My hands are warm and heavy. My hands are warm and heavy." As you do this, focus on the sensation of warmth in the hands and the sensation of heaviness.

Allow yourself to feel the warmth and heaviness as you repeat, "My hands are warm and heavy. My hands are warm and heavy."

Now focus on your feet as your heart rate slows and your muscles relax. Say to yourself, "My feet are warm and heavy. My feet are warm and heavy."

Let yourself concentrate on these sensations of relaxation as your feet feel warmth and heaviness. After a few moments experiencing the sensations of warmth and heaviness, reorient yourself to the room and open your eyes.

After completing this exercise, ask yourself, "Did I notice any change?" Even the first time, some people experience a very intense change in perception. For others, the change is less intense, with only heat or heaviness predominant. That's fine for now, as we'll expand on these experiences in a moment, but in just doing this one simple exercise, you have begun the process of learning that you control the responses of the autonomic nervous system.

For many people, the first time I guide them through a complete series of autogenic suggestions is empowering. They immediately feel a change and immediately recognize their own ability to control sensations of heat, heaviness, calmness, or coolness. What type of person benefits from such a practice? Irritable bowel syndrome patients, pain management patients, and patients in just about every medical setting.

A more profound question is this: If you can control sensations of coolness, warmth, and heaviness, do you also have the ability to control pain? Or comfort? Or healing? Or grief? Can you create happiness? Thinness? Can you create confidence or increase your resolve? This can be used in so many ways.

An initial program for autogenic training:

Again, sit in a meditative posture. I prefer to sit on a chair with the spine erect and the eyes closed. At first, you may need to keep the eyes open as you read these instructions, but soon you will commit them to memory and be able to close the eyes.

This self-hypnosis process consists of several phrases which you will repeat out loud three times. As you say each phrase, allow yourself to experience the sensations described. Many people ask me what the solar plexus is. The solar plexus refers to what some call "the pit of the stomach." It's both a scientific term, specifically describing a nerve center in the body, and a metaphysical term referring to the central place where energy resides. In personal training, this is the "core" area where important muscles and nerves join together to work in unison to promote maximum functioning.

"My right arm is heavy and warm." (Repeat three times.)

"My left arm is heavy and warm." (Repeat three times.)

"My arms are heavy and warm." (Repeat three times.)

"My neck and shoulders are heavy." (Repeat three times.)

"My heartbeat is calm and regular." (Repeat three times.)

"My left leg is heavy and warm." (Repeat three times.)

"My right leg is heavy and warm." (Repeat three times.)

"My legs are heavy and warm." (Repeat three times.)

"My solar plexus is warm and comfortable." (Repeat three times.)

"My forehead is cool." (Repeat three times.)

"I am at peace." (Repeat three times.)

As you expand the length of your self-hypnosis sessions and begin to combine methods, focusing on your breath becomes very important. We need to link the mental and physical aspects of relaxation. When we combine autogenic phrases with breathing, we can easily achieve deep states of relaxation. Imagine that your heart space is a vessel that holds all the energy taken in from each breath. With each exhalation, you let go of whatever old energy or thoughts you've been carrying around with you, allowing yourself to truly relax into the present moment.

For my client, who had lost his son, adding self-hypnosis to the dream analysis gave him a greater level of control. Instead of looking for the messages, he was open to a panoramic perspective on the experiences. He recognized that a specific message from his son not only might never be found but that, in some ways, it was no longer important to him. How did this change occur? By adding the autogenic practice to his dream analysis, he began to learn how to deeply relax, creating an inner environment of safety and peace. This allowed him to sleep better, dream differently, and experience his waking life in new ways. As he learned to trust the self-hypnosis process, new insights began to emerge. In a very short amount of time, he was able to start processing his grief and loss in a meaningful way, something that, to this point, had eluded him.

If you have never practiced the many different approaches to self-hypnosis that the research says are highly effective, you can learn more in both of my books on the subject. *The Seven Most Effective Methods of Self-Hypnosis* teaches strategies, like the one above, for various forms of self-hypnosis, and my other book, *The Self-Hypnosis Solution,* teaches applications to a variety of issues and experiences. I strongly suggest that one of the things that can make dream analysis panoramic—that is holistic and transcends our nighttime and daytime experiences—is the development of self-hypnosis. This can be done by practicing specific phrases, focusing on the breath, and allowing yourself to drift off into a deep state of relaxation. Self-hypnosis allows you to explore your dream world as well as your inner self.

Self-hypnosis is also a great tool for getting better sleep, recalling dreams, and paying closer attention to our subconscious mind and the myriad of thoughts that each of us has every day. In addition to the autogenic strategy above, you can also follow this easy six-part process to guide yourself into the resources state of hypnosis. Do this before going to bed at night and do it consistently, and I promise you will see the results.

1) Find a comfortable place to practice self-hypnosis. This can be a chair, the floor, or even your bed. You can use this process at any time, but at night it can help carry you quite efficiently to dreamland.

2) Make sure you are comfortable and relaxed. Close your eyes and take a few deep breaths. Focus on the feeling of your breath going in and out as if you were watching a wave roll in and out with each breath.

3) As you focus on your breath, start to introduce positive autogenic phrases that are simple to remember but important reminders, such as "I am relaxed and comfortable," or "I accept the present moment mindfully," or "I am open to new learnings and new possibilities."

4) Now that you have your positive phrases in place, start to focus on different body parts. Start at the top of your head and work down. Relax each muscle as you go, using

simple commands such as "My forehead is relaxed" or "My jaw is loose and comfortable."

5) Once all muscles are relaxed, take a few more deep breaths and allow yourself to drift into deeper relaxation.

6) As you enter a deeper level of relaxation, visualize yourself in a safe, peaceful place. This could be a place where you have been before, a place you would like to go, or even a place of your own creation. Allow the relaxation to envelop your body and mind.

If you are practicing during the daytime, following a few minutes of deep relaxation after step six, reorient to the floor below you and the room around you and open the eyes with a smile on your face. If you are doing this at night, let that relaxation turn into deep sleep, allowing yourself to set aside any pressure or stress and enjoy a good night of deep sleep.

With the practice of self-hypnosis, dream analysis becomes a powerful tool for exploring yourself from a new perspective. As we learn more about our inner landscape through dreams, it can help us find meaning in our lives and better understand why we feel the way we do. Self-hypnosis is not only an effective means of personal exploration, but it's also beneficial for those who have experienced loss or trauma and need to process their feelings in a healthier way. In both cases, incorporating self-hypnosis into dream analysis offers us many possibilities for creating change and finding peace. Through combining these two practices, you may uncover hidden answers that will provide insight into your life's journey so far.

Chapter 13
Metaphors in Our Dreams

To gain an expanded panoramic view from dreams, it's vital to understand metaphors and how, at a subconscious level, metaphors create meaning. When we turn our attention to dreams, metaphors can help us explore the dream world and understand what lies beneath the surface of our conscious mind. Dream analysis often relies heavily on metaphors to interpret the symbolism in a dream and uncover hidden feelings, fears, or desires. By looking at certain objects or scenarios in a dream as metaphorical expressions of unseen emotions, we can enrich ourselves and find clarity in our own thoughts and feelings. Metaphors also provide an effective way of understanding a person's inner world and giving them respite from their immediate issues by allowing them to think outside the box. In this way, metaphors can be used as powerful tools for self-reflection and growth.

How can you identify the metaphors your subconscious mind is revealing in your sleep? The first step is to pay attention to the setting and characters in your dream. What objects or people appear in your dream? Try to identify symbols that could be interpreted metaphorically, such as a bridge or a road that could symbolize progress or a journey. Pay attention to the emotions you experience during the dream and how those feelings relate to your life outside of sleep. Are there any recurring images, ideas, or situations that stand out?

In the panoramic dream analysis approach, we do not ascribe a preconceived meaning to any aspect of a dream. Rather, we allow the dreamer to find the meaning that's important to them. What this means is that what you think a dream means is exactly what the dream means. This is important as we look at metaphors because only the dreamer can decide what a metaphor in their dream represents.

What is interesting is that metaphors occur across all languages and that all cultures use metaphors as a way to express and explain ideas. This suggests that our subconscious mind is using the same language of metaphor in our dreams, regardless of our cultural background or language. By understanding these metaphors and interpreting them through the lens of dream analysis, we can uncover deeper meanings about ourselves and our innermost thoughts and feelings. Metaphors provide a powerful tool for self-reflection, allowing us to explore the hidden messages within our dreams and find clarity in our lives.

In any stage of the HEART process, metaphors may become apparent. One way to find them is to look for repeating patterns or symbols that appear in the dream. This can help to uncover hidden emotions, fears, and desires that may be influencing our behavior in waking life. Another approach is to consider what objects, characters, and situations are present in the dream, as metaphors are often included in dreams as a way of expressing deeper meaning. By taking a closer look at these images and exploring how they relate to your life outside of sleep, you can learn more about yourself and find clarity by interpreting their metaphorical meanings.

Metaphors in hypnotherapy, psychology, and dream analysis provide a powerful tool for exploring the unconscious mind and finding clarity in our thoughts and feelings. By understanding what lies beneath the surface of our waking life, we can find deeper meaning in our own dreams. Taking advantage of this opportunity to explore the inner workings of your subconscious mind is an effective way to discover new perspectives on life and resolution about how you feel, think, and act. Once you have identified the metaphors that are present in your dream, use them as doorways to discovering more about yourself and your own unique worldview.

Here are a few examples of metaphorical dreams:

Life is like a box of chocolates: In this dream, the box of chocolates symbolizes the many life paths and choices available to us. This metaphor reminds us that each choice we make holds a different flavor and that all experiences can be enjoyed and savored in their own unique way.

Life is like a roller coaster: This metaphor suggests that life has its ups and downs, but it also implies that there's a thrill to be found in the journey. A dreamer I worked with interpreted this to mean that although life can be unpredictable and challenging, it's important to appreciate the beauty of the ride.

Life is like a game of chess: This dream metaphor encourages us to think strategically and plan ahead in order to make wise decisions. It also suggests that we have the power to take control of our lives and direct our own paths with careful consideration.

When looking at metaphors in dreams, it's crucial to remember that they're not literal interpretations of reality. By understanding their symbolic meaning, however, you can gain insight into your thoughts and feelings on a deeper level. As you explore these metaphors in your dreams, ponder how they relate to your waking life; this way, you can uncover new perspectives about yourself.

Once you've identified the metaphors in your dream, it's important to explore what these symbols mean for you on a personal level. Make connections between the metaphor and how it relates to your life; this will help uncover deeper meanings and insights about yourself. Additionally, consider how the metaphors might be offering advice or guidance about how you can move forward in your life with confidence. Through careful interpretation of these symbols, you can achieve valuable insight into yourself that will ultimately lead to greater self-growth and understanding.

Remember, someone else may have a similar dream, yet for cultural, experiential, or personal reasons, the metaphor may have a different meaning for them. The great thing about panoramic dream analysis is that you get to discover the metaphors in your dreams and ascribe meaning to them. You can't be wrong! So have fun exploring and interpreting the metaphors in your dreams, and may they bring you clarity and insight into yourself. This is crucial because many of us feel that others have a sense of control over our emotions, our lives, our choices, and even our dreams, but understanding and interpreting the metaphors in our dreams allows us to take back that power.

Chapter 14
Free Association in Dream Analysis

One of the best ways to gain a panoramic vantage point—one where you can see everything and discover new truths about your dreams—is to use free association, which is the technique of Sigmund Freud. Freud wrote extensively about dreams. He even wrote a whole book specifically about dream analysis. You can use the HEART process and then apply some of Freud's ideas to gain even more insight and application. This is one of the great things about the panoramic dream analysis approach; it's multi-theoretical, which means you can continue to work on any dream with a wide-angle lens view, and you can use multiple methods to expand this awareness.

Freud believed that when you free-associate your dreams, you get a clearer view of your unconscious. He argued that when someone experiences a dream, they often experience it in terms of symbolic images and feelings that are associated with the dream's content.

This can be seen as a kind of visual language for understanding what our subconscious is trying to tell us about ourselves. By exploring the symbolism within these dreams, we're able to uncover deeper insights into our own personal struggles and desires.

Free association also helps us see the value of our dreams by connecting them to other ideas and events in our life. It allows us to make connections between seemingly disparate elements in order to arrive at new understandings and perspectives on any given situation. Through this process, we may be able to break through our own barriers and biases in order to have a deeper understanding of our dreams.

In short, free association is an invaluable tool for dream analysis. It enables us to access the unconscious depths of our psyche and discover more about ourselves than we ever thought possible. By using this method, we can get an expansive perspective on any dream—one that goes far beyond what we initially see first. This can lead to profound insights into who we are and how our dreams are truly speaking to us. In the end, free association may be the key to unlocking your full potential as both a dreamer and an analyst!

In therapy, a session of free association surrounding a dream might look a lot like this: A therapist might ask their client to identify the elements in their dream, what feelings it evokes, and why (this is something you did in the HEART process). Then they could walk them through free association as a way of discovering new insights about the dream's content. Through this process, clients may access reflections on past events or experiences that can help them find resolution or meaning within current life issues. This can provide an invaluable tool for self-discovery and personal growth.

Free association is done by simply allowing your mind to wander and make connections between things. You can do this in various ways, such as freewriting, doodling, brainstorming, or self-hypnosis with a partner or by oneself. Through this process of exploration and association, you can arrive at new discoveries that may not have been apparent before using the HEART process. The idea is to allow your unconscious mind to take charge and see where it goes without judgment or preconceived ideas about what should happen next.

Free Association Practice Exercise:

Begin by completing the HEART process worksheet and identifying all the elements of your recent dream, including the first-person narration and the emotions, archetypes, symbols, and truths that surround that dream.

Then free-associate by writing or speaking aloud (or a combination of both) any ideas that come to mind when thinking about the dream elements. Don't be afraid to think outside the box and explore any associations, no matter how strange they appear at first.

This exercise will help you uncover deeper insights into your own subconscious and can reveal truths that may have been hidden from plain view.

I think it's best to free-associate with paper and pen when doing self-analysis. You can write words, doodle, or draw what comes to mind. I find that this is a great way to capture my ideas and reflect on them later while also letting the process of free association flow. You do not need to be an artist to do this. I frequently free-associate by drawing pictures, yet my own art abilities are limited to stick figures and sunshine drawn in a corner with lines sticking out. This work is for you; it's not for someone else. It's your opportunity to use a creative element to expand your analysis, get a broader perspective, and see the whole panoramic view.

Another way to practice free association, especially if you are a visual person, is to use visualization or guided imagery. Visualize the dream elements and then allow your mind to freely explore any thoughts that come to mind as they pertain to the dream. Allow yourself time in this visualization space without judgment or expectation of what might come up. This form of exploration can be particularly helpful for accessing deeper levels of our unconscious thought patterns, analyzing them, and bringing them into awareness. In fact, this is a form of self-hypnosis or meditation and can be used to access the deeper levels of our psyche.

You can also work with a dream analyst or a friend to practice free association. One way to do this is to give them your HEART worksheet and have them read each answer while you then respond with whatever comes to mind. This can be a fun, interactive way to explore your dream elements and uncover new insights, especially if you're sharing with a close friend, partner, or spouse.

The goal of free association is to unlock subconscious thought patterns, have greater insight into our own psyche, and get in touch with our intuition. Through this practice, we can receive clarity on life issues or struggles that we're facing, discover hidden talents and abilities within ourselves, and find resolve to current problems. Free association also allows us to develop self-awareness by tapping into our unconscious mind and processing emotions and thoughts in order to better understand ourselves.

It may seem weird when you do free association as if somehow there is an expected answer. However, by letting go and getting into the flow of the process, you will discover what at first appears to be a random answer regarding the other elements of the HEART worksheets or your other dreams, connections, and correlations (that were not so obvious before) start to emerge.

Free association and dream analysis are powerful tools for anyone interested in exploring their unconscious mind and uncovering the hidden depths of their psyche. This method can be used to find answers to life's questions, develop self-awareness, gain clarity on difficult issues, or simply enjoy the process of exploration and discovery. So go ahead, grab some paper and a pen or sit down with a friend and use free association to explore your inner world! No matter which method you choose, free association is a powerful tool for dream analysis and personal growth. By allowing yourself the freedom to explore your own thoughts and ideas without judgment, it can open up opportunities for understanding your dreams in ways you never imagined possible!

By combining free association with dream analysis, you can achieve a greater understanding of yourself on a mental, emotional, and spiritual level. With practice, you'll be able to unlock the hidden meanings in your dreams, explore new creative outlets, and develop more self-awareness. So go ahead and explore! What do you have to lose? By exploring our dreams with free association, we can gain access to insight from our unconscious self and discover new ways of understanding ourselves and our lives. Combined with Freud's dream analysis techniques, this process provides an invaluable tool for getting greater awareness of our inner workings. Through it, we can move beyond the surface-level interpretations of our dreams and uncover deeper meanings.

Another method of exploring your dreams that draws from a psychoanalytic tradition is called "image streaming." Although our dreams are multi-sensorial, which means we also smell, taste, hear, touch, and feel in our dreams, image streaming is an exercise that focuses on visual images from your dreams. To do this, you can think back to a dream and try to recall as much detail as possible about the visuals. Then write down these images, being sure to include any feelings or emotions connected with them (you have done this with your HEART worksheet).

In image streaming, although focused on the visual elements, you will describe every detail and element out loud as quickly as possible. You can do this with a partner or even dictate it into your phone and allow it to flow without judgment or analysis. This process can help you uncover the unconscious messages of your dream as well as any potential insights or understandings into your life.

Dr. Win Wenger was a pioneer in the area of image streaming, and he believed it could enhance creativity, accelerate learning, and even improve physical health.

Panoramic Dream Analysis

The simple image streaming process he shared can help you have greater insight into your dreams as well as uncover potential insights and understanding in all areas of your life.

To practice image streaming, follow this process:

1. Pick a dream that's been troubling you in the past and focus on it in detail.
2. Write down the images from your dream, along with any related feelings or emotions.
3. Read through your list of images out loud and as quickly as possible without judgment or analysis.
4. After completing this process, explore how these images might relate to current issues and situations in your life.
5. Reflect on what insights you have received from this exercise and how it can help further your understanding of yourself and your life.

By utilizing the tools of free association, dream analysis, and image streaming, we can learn more about our unconscious mind so that we can live a more meaningful life. Through this exploration, we can uncover our true potential, find new creative outlets, and make more informed choices in life. So go ahead and try it out today! Who knows what kind of insights you might discover.

Chapter 15
Discovering Patterns and Connecting Dreams

Dream analysis is an important part of Jungian psychology, developed by Swiss psychiatrist Carl Jung. Jung was a contemporary of Freud; at one point, they even worked together. Freud, however, saw dreams as expressions of our repressed desires, while Jung saw them as having a greater significance. To him, dreams were doorways to the subconscious and held important symbols that could help us understand our lives better and make sense of unresolved issues.

One of the techniques for analyzing dreams was to look for patterns in them. According to Jung, looking for patterns in your dreams can give you insight into what's going on in your life at that time. He believed that certain themes or images kept appearing in our dreams when we had something unresolved in our lives, such as feelings of guilt or anxiety. For example, if you keep dreaming about being chased by a monster or an animal, it might suggest underlying feelings of fear or insecurity that need to be addressed. According to Jung, dreams are a direct way of expressing our innermost desires and can be used to get an accurate understanding of our lives. In panoramic dream analysis, our goal is to discover the full view, seeing every side and angle of our dreams, but most importantly, putting it within the context of a larger picture of meaning and finding applications from our dreams to our wide-awake world.

Jungian techniques for dream analysis involve exploring symbols in dreams as well as identifying recurring patterns or themes in them. In other words, Jungian approaches let us connect seemingly unrelated dreams to one another. This is the value of a dream diary or the regular practice of completing the HEART worksheets and making a journal out of them. To practice the Jungian approach, we can try to draw connections between our dream symbols and our waking life. We might also try to look for patterns in the way our dreams develop over time or even compare them with the stories of other people's dreams.

One of the best ways to discern these patterns is to look through the HEART worksheets and write down on another piece of paper those emotions that occur most often, the symbols, archetypes, or images that occur most often, and note the people that appear most often. Who appears in your dreams other than you on a regular basis? What do those people symbolize to you? What are the common themes or images in your dreams? Do they have any special meaning for you?

Panoramic Dream Analysis

By connecting our dream symbols and patterns with our waking life, we can get a clear understanding of what's going on within us. When we connect the dots between our dreams, it allows us to make sense of them and see how dreaming can help us uncover our unconscious motivations and needs. Dream analysis is a powerful tool for attaining an understanding of ourselves and discovering solutions to problems in our lives.

To connect the dreamwork to the daytime world, you can ask yourself these twelve questions, all based on noticing patterns and connections between multiple dreams:

1. How do my dreams connect with each other?
2. What are the common themes or images in my dreams?
3. Are there any special symbols that keep appearing in my dreams?
4. How do my dreams fit into the larger pattern of what's going on in my life right now?
5. Are there any unresolved issues from the past that might be surfacing in these dreams?
6. What feelings are being expressed by the people and situations in my dream?
7. What solutions might be available to me based on what I've learned from analyzing these patterns and connections between multiple dreams?
8. Do these patterns and connections between multiple dreams give me any insights into my behavior or attitudes?
9. What might this dream be telling me about my relationships with other people?
10. Is there anything I can learn from the way in which my dreams progress over time?

11. How might these dreams help me to understand myself better and find a new perspective on life?
12. Are there any creative solutions I can find using what I've learned from analyzing the pattern of my dreams?

Answering these questions is an important step in understanding how our unconscious mind works and how we can use our dreams to gain insight into our lives and uncover potential solutions to unresolved problems or feelings. Panoramic dream analysis allows us to explore the full view of our dreams and uncover new insights into our inner lives. It's a powerful tool for personal growth and self-discovery, and with practice can help us make sense of the seemingly random images that appear in our dreams.

The Thirty-Day Panoramic Dream Challenge

Let me encourage you to take the thirty-day dream analysis challenge and keep a daily HEART sheet for each dream you have in a month. Then, at the end of that month, go through all your dream sheets and see if you can detect any patterns or common themes. Allow yourself to get creative with connecting the dots between multiple dreams. This exercise will help you to have a better understanding of Jungian techniques and how they can be applied to your personal life.

There is another contribution by Jung that I think is also important. Jung wrote about the "collective consciousness," which is the idea that there is a collective unconscious shared by all humanity. This idea supports the notion that we're all connected and that our dreams can be used as a way to tap into this collective wisdom allowing us to attain insight from universal experiences.

Over the years, I've had numerous partners, professional and personal, with whom I've shared my dreams. Each time I did so, I was amazed at how our collective understanding of the dream images expanded and revealed new depths of insight. But even more amazing has been introducing the idea of "dreaming together," which is an attempt at some level to create shared lucid dreams (lucid dreams are when the dreamer is aware that they're dreaming and can often control the dream) and to co-create dreams I could then discuss and analyze with my partner. This has been an exciting experience, and it reinforces the idea of a collective unconscious, as well as our interconnectedness with each other and nature.

Jungian techniques for dream analysis can be an incredibly powerful tool for personal growth and self-discovery. With practice and patience, we can start to make sense of the seemingly random images that appear in our dreams and uncover new insights into our inner lives. By connecting the dots between multiple dreams, using the HEART method, and exploring the collective unconscious, we can learn valuable knowledge about ourselves and those around us. Dream analysis is an ancient art that's still relevant today and can be a great source of nourishment for the mind, body, and soul.

Chapter 16
Nightmares

Jill called me, desperate for a solution to her nightmares. For the past eighteen months, she had experienced increasing nightmares, which she attributed to stress and trauma in her life. She said that she found the nightmares so overwhelming and debilitating that they left her drained of energy throughout the day and made it difficult for her to concentrate on anything else.

Some of her nightmares were so painful to her that she was afraid to go to bed every night. She was at her wits' end. That's when she called me. And she was ready to try anything I recommended to get some relief.

I suggested that she consider dream analysis as a way of processing the underlying emotions attached to her nightmares. Panoramic dream analysis is beneficial to those distressed by nightmares, even PTSD-related nightmares, recurring nightmares, and nightmares that feel too terrifying to bear.

Panoramic dream analysis can be used to identify the bigger picture of the nightmare experience, reframe the experience, and find new meaning in the nightmares. This can be a way to cope with them and eventually decrease the power of a nightmare. It involves exploring the symbolic imagery in dreams as well as the emotions associated with them. By understanding why we dream certain things, we can begin to make sense of our nightmares and see what they mean for us on an emotional level. This knowledge can then be used to develop coping strategies that allow us to confront our fears and eventually stop having recurring nightmares.

For Jill, our goal was to accomplish three things. First, to help her reframe the experience. Yes, the nightmares were scary and distressing. But no matter how bad the nightmares were, she always woke up and woke up safe in her bed. This is a powerful truth that everyone with nightmares needs to focus on. No matter how difficult a dream is, 100 percent of the time, it's a dream, and it ends. In therapy, it's important for people to learn that feelings are not the same thing as facts, and in dream analysis, it's important to remember that dreams are not facts. This reframe can allow a nightmare sufferer to get perspective and distance from the dream.

Our second goal was to put some space between Jill and her dreams. When we dream, the dreamer is not just observing a dream but participating in it. Through panoramic dream analysis and using the HEART worksheets, Jill was able to explore her dreams in a different way and do so mindfully. One of the great benefits of the HEART worksheets is that they cultivate mindfulness by encouraging dreamers to become aware of their feelings or responses in the moment.

Finally, our third goal was to help Jill develop insight and self-compassion around her nightmares. By understanding what the nightmares meant on an emotional level, she could learn how to respond differently and cultivate a more compassionate relationship with herself. Through panoramic dream analysis, Jill began to create stories that made sense of her dreams and connected them to personal experiences from her life. In time, this process allowed her to achieve new insights into her dreams and use these newfound understandings as a way of cultivating peace and acceptance within herself.

In the HEART process, the R stands for rehearsal. Analyzing nightmares requires that this step of the process is really focused on. The opportunity that arises by focusing on the rehearsal aspect is to determine what experiential learning the dreamer can take from the nightmare. Not all dreams are nightmares but for those who have them rehearsing how to react in the moment of a nightmare or difficult dream and creating new pathways for thinking about them is helpful in order to acquire understanding into their lives.

Image rehearsal techniques can be used in dream analysis work, in therapy, and even in self-analysis. This involves focusing on the dream as if it were a movie and then picturing new endings or outcomes for the dream sequence. In Jill's case, she was able to imagine how her dream could end differently—with her feeling empowered rather than scared by the experience. By rehearsing different outcomes for her nightmares, Jill was able to discover what these nightmares may be trying to tell her about herself and how she can feel more in control of them.

Rehearsal is part of the HEART process because, for both nightmares and other dreams, it can show a pathway to the next step of testing, transferring, and trusting. Testing involves validating the new understanding of the dreamer and their nightmare by incorporating this new insight into everyday life. Transferring is a process in which the dreamer learns to apply the information they received from their nightmares to other areas of their lives and experiences. Finally, trusting means trusting that when we face our fears in dreams, it can make us stronger as individuals as we get fresh perspectives on situations we may be facing in waking life.

In Jill's case, she was able to use dream analysis to better understand her feelings around her nightmares, develop coping strategies for dealing with them, and eventually stop having them altogether. Through panoramic dream analysis and the HEART process, she was able to both reframe the experience of her nightmare and learn how to become more resilient in the face of fear. By understanding and exploring the meaning behind her dreams, Jill was able to form a better sense of self-compassion and trust that she has what it takes to face anything life throws at her.

Overall, panoramic dream analysis is an effective tool for helping those who suffer from recurrent nightmares. It provides an opportunity to explore dreams safely, understand their meanings on deeper levels, reframe negative experiences, create new pathways of thinking around them, and cultivate self-compassion. The process of uncovering the dreamer's inner resources can be an empowering experience and ultimately lead to increased resilience when faced with difficult or challenging situations.

One theory as to why we have nightmares is that they are produced by the subconscious mind as a way to rehearse difficult emotions, experiences, and issues so that in the safety of our sleep, we can practice how to respond in real life. Through panoramic dream analysis, we can use these insights to help us reimagine our nightmares and eventually stop having them altogether.

One of the key elements in the process is acceptance. Acceptance does not imply we like something, want it to happen, or are happy with a situation, but it does mean that we understand the reality of our experience. The HEART process encourages dreamers to be receptive to their dreams and emotions, allowing them to observe what arises without judgment or resistance. Through this practice, the dreamer is able to recreate the nightmare in order for them to take away valuable insights from the experience that can help them reduce fear and anxiety associated with nightmares.

When dreamers accept that nightmares are a part of their experience, something amazing happens. The nightmares begin to hold no power. This is what I call "The Paradox." I have shared this message in my TEDx Talk, in therapy sessions, and in some of my previous books:

THE PARADOX

Is when something is ACCEPTED as just being what it is, it then holds no POWER. Depression, loneliness, hunger, fear, or even withdrawal become unimportant when accepted.

When it becomes unimportant, it becomes just... what is.

It is something experienced rather than something I fight or hate or am restricted by or obsessed with. I can find FREEDOM from suffering.

Depression is not a problem. Hunger is not a problem. Withdrawal is not a problem. Loneliness is not a problem. It is only a problem if I make it one. These things let me know I am a human being, NOT a human doing.

Happiness would suck if life had no depression.

Security would suck if we had no sense of fear to put it in perspective.

Difficult times and experiences are a part of any valued path. Difficulty and even pain are not to be avoided if one wants a truly meaningful life. They are simply things to accept because in acceptance, we give them no power to control, and they become the pathway to being:

A FULL HUMAN BEING PARTICIPATING FULLY IN LIFE.

This paradox certainly applies to those who experience nightmares. Through panoramic dream analysis, we learn that nightmares can be an opportunity for growth and understanding, allowing us to create stories that make sense of our dreams. We can use these newfound understandings to cultivate peace and acceptance within ourselves. In the end, this process has the power to stop nightmares once and for all.

Dreams are not meant to be feared but treasured as a powerful tool for self-discovery. By recognizing their value and learning how to work with them in healthy ways through panoramic dream analysis, it's possible to transform fear into freedom and nightmares into opportunities for growth. Through this process, we can reclaim the power of our dreams and control our own destiny.

Dream analysis is not an overnight solution. However, over time it can prove transformative for those experiencing recurring nightmares. By learning how to pause and reflect on dreams, as well as look into their meaning, dreamers can begin to develop coping strategies that eventually help them stop having nightmares altogether. With the right tools and a bit of practice, Jill was able to take control of her dreams and begin living a life free from fear and terrorizing dreams. In time she was able to move beyond focusing on the nightmare itself and start enjoying the blissful state of deep sleep that we all deserve.

Chapter 17
Unlocking the Benefits of Your Dreams

By using the ideas in this book, your dreams will no longer be a mystery, and more importantly, they will become a resource that connects your nighttime creativity to your daytime success. Through panoramic dream analysis and the HEART process, you will develop a much deeper understanding of your dreams and be able to use them to help you make important decisions in your life.

This book has been a great journey for us both—one that will probably continue far into the future as more dream secrets are uncovered. Whether you're using dream analysis for personal or professional reasons, one thing is certain: Dreams can open portals of insight and understanding that are otherwise unavailable to us in our waking lives.

I have some resources for you that I want to share. First, on my website at www.PanoramicDreams.com, you can print the HEART worksheets, access some video tutorials, and take a deeper look into dream analysis. and unlock the power of your dreams. Many of these resources on my website are free for you to access, and I want you to use them and make the most out of your dream discoveries.

Second, I have a private social media group which you can join, and it's a great place to share your dreams, ask others for support, and discover new ways to apply the HEART process to gain a panoramic view of your experiences. The link to our group is on my website, but you can also go to Facebook and search for the "Panoramic Dream Analysis" group.

What can dream analysis do for you? It can unlock many profound benefits:

1. Analyzing dream content can help to provide clarity on our goals and ambitions, guiding us toward potential paths to pursue in order to achieve success or happiness in life.
2. Examining the emotions experienced within a dream world can inform actions taken in real life as we unravel the underlying meaning behind our subconscious thought processes.
3. Making sense of dreams provides an opportunity to gain control over aspects of life that have previously felt difficult or out of reach due to a lack of insight into one's own behavior patterns.
4. Dream analysis allows us to receive messages from higher powers or sources beyond our conscious awareness, helping us find solace in times of stress while offering guidance on unresolved issues.

5. Interpreting the symbolism contained within our dreamscape gives us a chance to step outside of ourselves and become more mindful and aware of how our thoughts and decisions affect others around us, creating a greater understanding between all parties involved for everyone's benefit.
6. Interpreting dreams can help us better understand our wants and needs in life. By analyzing the symbolism in our dreams, we can gain insight into ourselves and identify motivations for pursuing certain goals or desires.
7. Dream analysis can help us uncover hidden sources of stress or conflict that might be holding us back from success in areas such as work, relationships, and personal development.
8. Understanding the meaning behind recurring dreams or nightmares can give us insight into patterns of behavior that no longer serve us and need to be addressed.
9. Analyzing our dreams may provide clues about how to improve our relationships with others by helping us understand what we expect from them and why they may be failing to meet those expectations.
10. Working through dream analysis can open up new ways of seeing the world around us and offer ideas for potential solutions to current problems that may not have been considered previously.
11. Analyzing dream symbols can help us recognize patterns of self-sabotage that keep us stuck in destructive cycles and free ourselves from these repeated behaviors and thought processes.
12. Exploring our dreams can inform future decision-making by indicating which paths will lead to greater happiness and fulfillment or encourage more caution

if signs point to a potentially risky outcome if we take a certain route.
13. Dream symbolism gives us an opportunity to explore our creative abilities without fear of failure, leading to innovative solutions that would otherwise never have been conceived due to hesitation or a lack of confidence in one's abilities in waking life scenarios.
14. Interpreting the imagery within a dreamscape can offer clarity pertaining to questions we have about ourselves, others, or certain events—providing helpful insights into issues that may have otherwise been difficult to solve on our own with logic alone.
15. Dreams act as a form of therapy, revealing unconscious fears, desires, doubts, anxieties, etc., all while being safely contained within an alternate reality we create where anything is possible!

With the ideas you have learned in this book, and the resources I've provided, either through self-analysis or working with a partner or even a professional, you can unlock the hidden depths of your subconscious and discover more about yourself, your inner motivations, and how you can best make progress toward achieving success or happiness in life. Using the HEART process as a foundation for dream analysis can help to create a safe space for personal growth through the exploration of one's own dreams. The possibilities are endless—dive in and enjoy the journey!

As you decode all the secrets that lie within your dream world, with panoramic dream analysis and the HEART process as tools at your disposal, you will find new ways to gain insight into yourself and uncover answers to questions that have been on your mind. Ultimately, this knowledge can help lead you to greater understanding, self-awareness, and wisdom—allowing you to make conscious decisions that are in line with your goals and values, being more mindful and heartful of how our thoughts and decisions affect others around us; and creating a greater understanding between all parties involved for everyone's benefit.

There's no limit to what we can learn from dream analysis—the only boundaries are those set by ourselves, so start today with the 30-Day Challenge. Print out the HEART worksheets from my website and begin a journey that will open all doors to success in areas such as work, relationships, and personal development. Happy travels!

Get Access to The Free Resources for
Dream Analysis at:

www.PanoramicDreams.com

Please leave a review for this book
at your favorite book seller!

Also, discover the many other book by Dr. Richard Nongard to help you achieve your goals and dreams by simply searching your favorite bookseller by name.

www.ingramcontent.com/pod-product-compliance
Lightning Source LLC
Chambersburg PA
CBHW061729070526
44583CB00024B/3063